IDENTITY

seeing
yourself
through
GOD'S
eyes

CONRAD HILARIO

DEDICATION

To my beautiful wife, Hilary, on our 15th
anniversary. I love you more than ever.

I'm so grateful to God for putting you in my life. You
are strong in the ways I am weak. Your belief in me
has spurred me to serve God with all my heart.

You have filled my life with happiness.

ACKNOWLEDGEMENTS

To my mentor, Dennis McCallum, who introduced me to my new identity in Christ. Reading your book, *Walking in Victory*, changed my life. Thank you for your investment over the years. I'm indebted to you.

Special thanks to my friend and editor, John Ross, who left my manuscript looking like a butcher's apron. Your constructive criticism helped me grow as a writer and helped elevate the content of this book.

Contents

A Simple Solution to a Complex Problem — 9

Seeing Yourself Through God's Eyes — 13

ONE. Holy + Blameless — 21

TWO. Sealed with the Spirit — 27

THREE. New Creation in Christ — 35

FOUR. Free from the Law — 41

FIVE. No Longer Slaves to Sin — 49

SIX. Forgiven — 57

SEVEN. Adopted Son or Daughter — 65

EIGHT. Child of God: Our Heavenly Father — 71

NINE. Child of God: Becoming Like Little Children — 77

TEN. Child of God: Receiving Loving Discipline — 85

ELEVEN. God's Friend — 91

TWELVE. God's Friend: Being a Good Friend — 97

THIRTEEN. Bearer of a New Name — 103

FOURTEEN. Bearer of God's Family Name — 109

FIFTEEN. One in Christ — 115

SIXTEEN. Body of Christ — 121

SEVENTEEN. Bride of Christ — 127

EIGHTEEN. Temple of God — 133

NINETEEN. Royal Priesthood — 139

TWENTY. Salt + Light — 145

TWENTY-ONE. Citizen of Heaven — 151

TWENTY-TWO. Temporary Resident — 157

TWENTY-THREE. Ambassador — 163

TWENTY-FOUR. Not of This World — 169

TWENTY-FIVE. Servant of Christ — 175

TWENTY-SIX. Combatant: Freedom Fighter — 183

TWENTY-SEVEN. Combatant: The Battle of the Mind — 191

TWENTY-EIGHT. Conformed to the Image of Christ — 199

A Simple Solution to a Complex Problem

You could describe the current state of our culture in two words: identity crisis. Many young people today are creating an identity from social differences. Some look to race or ethnicity. For a growing number, identity is determined by one's gender or sexual orientation. Others build a sense of self from political or social causes.

More often people build their identity around things like achievement. In the classic movie, *Cool Runnings*, a Jamaican sprinter named Derice Bannock fails to qualify for the Summer Olympics. Desperate to compete, he forms the first Jamaican bobsled team in history with the help of disgraced American bobsledder Irving "Irv" Blitzer, played by John Candy. The Winter Olympic Committee stripped Irv of two gold medals for cheating years earlier.

After the Jamaican team qualifies to compete in the 1988 games, Derice asks Irv why he cheated.

"It's quite simple really," Irv answers. "I had to win."

He continues, "You see, Derice, I've made winning my whole life, and when you make winning your whole life, you have to keep winning no matter what."

Derice fires back in confusion, "You had two gold medals. You had it all!"

"Derice, a gold medal is a wonderful thing," Irv replies as Derice nods with approval. "But if you are not enough without it, you'll never be enough with it."

Derice asks, "Hey, coach, how will I know if I'm enough?"

Those who center their identity on success make their whole lives about winning. But it leaves them wondering: *How will I know I'm enough?*

Comparison fuels our drive for success. We want what others have. We dream of their recognition. We long for their wealth. We aspire to their success because it will add to our cachet. That's why we often feel dissatisfied with our work. We're not manufacturing a good or service, we're manufacturing a sense of self.

Others form their identity around money and possessions. Researchers asked Harvard students to choose between two options: make $90,000 per year while others earn $45,000, or make $180,000 a year while others earn $450,000. The majority chose the first option.[1] That means most people would rather make half as much, just to have more than others.

Why do we compare our material wealth to others? Wealth assigns us a certain status. It places us within a layer of society that defines most aspects of our lives. It allows us to move into specific neighborhoods. It gives us access to certain social circles. It opens more opportunities. All these factors determine our status — and status is another way of measuring ourselves against others.

People find a variety of other ways to define themselves. They establish their worth on romantic love and family, or power and influence. or perceived competence and peer approval, or fitness and physical beauty, or the emotional dependence of others, or even success in Christian ministry.

The trouble with constructing an identity on any of these things is that it can topple at any moment. It's based on comparisons, or it balances on things that can be taken from you. It was never supposed to be this way.

Human autonomy is the taproot from which all sins originate. The first act of defiance against God was a step toward self-reliance. Humans no longer looked to God for leadership. Instead, humanity chose to carry the crushing load of leading itself.

Casting off God's leadership means bearing the burden of meeting our own needs. That's why we feel more relief than elation when we attain long-term goals. That's why our family and friends never live up to our demands. That's why worries about our finances drains our energy. We are trying to meet our needs through possessions, people and performance.

Now, these things aren't inherently bad. As author Timothy Keller explains:

> The human heart takes *good things* like a successful career, love, material possessions, even family, and turns them into *ultimate things*. Our hearts deify them as the center of our lives, because, we think, they can give us significance and security, safety and fulfillment.[2]

God solved this complex problem with a simple solution: He's given us a new identity. The only way to access this is through his son, Jesus. Our disregard for God not only gives us the responsibility of meeting our own needs, it also condemns us. And yet, God's love for us drove him to sacrifice his one and only son on a cross, so that he could forgive us and offer us a relationship with him. All we need to do is receive Jesus' death as payment for our sins. The moment we do this, our status changes. Scripture assures us that "to those who believed in his name, he gave the right to become children of God" (John 1:12, NASB).

Who you are determines what you do. Something as simple as knowing that God sees you as his son or daughter will transform your life, and this is just one aspect of who you are in Christ. As you discover your new identity and begin to see yourself through God's eyes, you will view yourself and reality different.

Seeing Yourself Through God's Eyes

Have you ever stumbled upon a landmark in your neighborhood that was hiding in plain sight? Twice a week, I drive past an empty building that sits across the street from one of our meeting spaces near The Ohio State University. I've passed this building hundreds of times. Last year, I found out it's on the National Register of Historic Places. It was the first junior high school in America. The famous architect who designed Ohio Stadium — home of The Ohio State Buckeyes — drafted the plans for this building. For years, I never knew this building had historical importance. Now, I'm reminded of it every time I drive by.

"In Christ" is perhaps one of those phrases you see but never notice while reading the Bible. And yet, it's a major emphasis. When God wants to call attention to something, he repeats it.

The phrase "in Christ" or "in Him" appears more than 150 times in the New Testament. However, you almost never hear Christians mention it when talking about spiritual growth.

Most books on spiritual transformation focus on exposing false ideologies, uncovering misplaced affections and confronting warped theology. No doubt, these distortions keep believers enslaved in self-destructive behavior. On the other hand, Scripture tells us that the heart of spiritual growth is embracing who we are in Christ.

I would argue that the lack of spiritual growth in the church today is largely a result of this dim awareness of our new identity. It isn't enough to tell yourself to stop doing something you know is wrong. It's essential to see who you are in Jesus.

PUT INTO CHRIST

God gives us a new identity the instant we place our faith in Jesus. The Apostle Paul assumes all believers should know this. "Don't you know that all of us who were baptized into Christ Jesus were baptized into his death?" (Romans 6:3). Now, most associate the word "baptize" with water baptism. But Paul must have written this with something else in mind. He's not talking about water baptism. If he was, it would suggest water baptism grants you salvation.

The word "baptize" contains a wide range of meaning. Ancient authors used the Greek verb to describe immersing or dipping an object.[3] The first-century Jewish historian, Josephus, used this verb in the context of dyeing. If you put a piece of fabric into a solution, it undergoes a chemical change. Fibers drink up the color and take on the properties of the dye.

That's what Paul describes here: God put you in Christ and therefore identifies you with him. Just as Jesus lived a life without blemish, God chose us *in him* to be holy and blameless (Ephesians 1:4). Just as "the Father loves the Son," God shows us the same love because he adopted us as sons and daughters *in Christ* (Ephesians 1:5). As Christian author Dennis McCallum puts it, "What is true of Christ is also true of us who are in Christ."[4]

Scripture uses dozens of metaphors to describe our new identity. It says we are like resident "aliens" in a foreign land (1 Peter 2:11). It calls us "ambassadors" for Christ in the world (2 Corinthians 5:20). It compares us to "living stones" God uses to build his "holy temple" (1 Peter 2:5).

Have you ever heard of a View-Master? It was a cherry red, plastic toy that looked like binoculars and came with cardboard photo reels. Each reel had a collection of pictures with a theme, like outer space or marine life. You would load a reel and look through the lenses. As light entered the viewer, it transformed each picture into a 3-D image. Pressing the lever advanced the reel to the next image. Similarly, as you advance through the pages of Scripture, each metaphor describing your new identity helps you to see how God views you in Christ.

The first major step you can take toward spiritual growth is to discover who you are in Christ. This book is devoted to helping you with this. Each chapter gives a short reflection about one aspect of your new identity. Why not devote the rest of this month to learning about who you are in Christ?

WHAT IS OUR PART?

Seeing these metaphors is not enough. We know lots of things, but they don't always change our lives. Our job is belief. Not just belief of any kind. Belief that draws confidence from what God says and puts it into action.

After we put the time into learning about our new identity, God calls on us to trust what he says about us in Christ. We need to see ourselves as God sees us. That's why Scripture urges us to "consider" ourselves dead to sin — our old way of life — and alive to God in Christ Jesus (Romans 6:11). The ancient Greek word for "consider" or "reckon" was an accounting term.

Not long ago, middle schools required students to take a life skills class.

To pass, you had to "reconcile" a checkbook. Before online banking, you had to hand calculate your balance because you couldn't look it up in real time. This exercise helped track spending and avoid overdrafts. Teachers would give students a sheet with several columns. One listed your deposits, withdrawals and issued checks. Another allowed you to add or subtract each from your starting amount. If you did everything right, the final balance on your sheet matched the balance on your bank statement. This helped you reckon how much money you thought you had with how much was really in the bank. It brought beliefs and reality into agreement.

Likewise, God wants us to reconcile what we think is true about ourselves and what he says is true of us. He wants to bring these into alignment. The more we see ourselves as God sees us, the more we become like Christ.

God also wants us to "present" ourselves to him in our new identity (Romans 6:13). It's not enough to see ourselves through God's eyes; we also must approach him as we are in Christ. This may seem simple, but it's not always easy.

Your identity in Christ is as fixed as the orbits of planets. How you feel about yourself does not change how God feels about you. Yet sometimes it's a struggle to draw near to him. We enter his presence with our eyes downcast during times of moral failure, even though God tells us that we are holy and blameless in his sight. It takes a certain amount of faith to come to him in our new identity.

HOW DOES A CHANGE OF IDENTITY CHANGE US?

All our deepest needs fall into two categories: the need for significance and the security of being loved. Without these we will shrivel. That's why we find ourselves grasping for something or someone to anchor our sense of identity.

Scripture tells us that God created us as dependent beings. He designed us to rely on him to meet all our needs. He also made us to be in a relationship with other people (Genesis 2:18). In other words, we need a relationship with God and human interaction to function the way he intended.

The Fall disrupted this delicate balance. Our sin disconnected us from God. This rupture caused us to place the full weight of our deepest needs onto the people around us. No wonder those around us feel crushed by our expectations. No wonder we feel crumpled by rejection. We are seeking to be filled by people in a way that only God can fill us.

Years ago, a young man in my small group was experiencing the short-term hysteria associated with being in love. He was dating a young woman who attended our group. His infatuation would take him to the heights of euphoria one moment, and cast him into the depths of despair the next. Panic would grip him if she didn't talk to him every day. Only a text message or a call would give him relief from the anxiety he felt. As in all great love stories, she dumped him.

He was crushed. For days, he would break down crying. A week later, he opened up to an older Christian about how he was feeling. The older believer offered him some comfort and then said, "As wonderful as this woman is, she will never fully meet your needs. She just wasn't built for that. In fact, no human being was built to do that. If you go on trying to find someone who will, you will be disappointed. The only one who can meet your deepest needs is God."

Our new status in Christ fills this deficit of love. I love the imagery the Apostle Paul uses in Romans 5, where he portrays God pouring out his love in our hearts. God loves us with the kind of love a parent has for a child. There is nothing a loving parent wouldn't do for their son or daughter. That type of love creates an environment of security.

Just think how trusting God would transform the way we relate to others.

It would unburden those around us. They would no longer suffer the draining relational demands of our co-dependency. Our entire mindset would shift toward others. We wouldn't look to take from those around us; we would look to give out of the overflow of love God has given us in Christ (1 John 4:11). We would cease trying to get others to meet our needs; instead, we would seek to meet the needs of others.

The Need for Significance

The fallen human heart knows no boundaries in its search for meaning apart from God. We try to leave an imprint on the world by creating beautiful works of art or inventing something that will make a lasting impact. We strive to leave a legacy. We feel this pressure to make our lives matter because time is running out.

The Pulitzer Prize-winning musical *Hamilton* intertwines the concepts of ambition and death. Alexander Hamilton talks about his dreams and boundless ambition in his song, "My Shot," but he's haunted by a darker thought: "I imagine death so much it feels more like a memory." Hamilton's rival, Aaron Burr, asks him, "Why do you write like you're running out of time?" Even the symbol of a gunshot illustrates the link between Hamilton's ambition and fear of death: A shot represents his drive ("I'm not throwing away my shot") and what kills him in a duel with Burr.

Creator Lin-Manuel Miranda explains how Hamilton's work ethic stems from his sense of mortality — and reveals that he shares the same motivation. "The ticking clock is loud in both our ears, and it sets us to work."

Who we are in Christ satisfies the tyrannical drive to define ourselves by our performance or people's approval. Only he can give you the significance you're striving to attain. God has given you more than eternal life, he's given you a new identity. You don't have to prove that you matter. Your new identity in Christ gives you value and worth — independent of your success or failure. You can quiet the voice that wakes you in the middle of the night and asks, *How will I know I'm enough?*

LASTING TRANSFORMATION

God has met your need for significance and security in Christ. This is the basis for spiritual growth. Any effort apart from this will lead to superficial change or failure. It's only as you discover what God says about you, trust him at his word and approach him with confidence that you will see transformation from the inside out.

ONE
Holy + Blameless

For he chose us in him before the creation of the world to be
holy and blameless in his sight.
EPHESIANS 1:4

Once you were alienated from God and were enemies in your
minds because of your evil behavior. But now he has reconciled
you by Christ's physical body through death to present you holy
in his sight, without blemish and free from accusation.
COLOSSIANS 1:21-22

"I, even I, am he who blots out your transgressions, for my own
sake, and remembers your sins no more."
ISAIAH 43:25

When modern people hear the word "holy," it's like the squeal of a rusty swing set. Many associate the term with someone who is "holier than thou." The Greek word for holy means something much different. It contains a wide range of meaning. Holy can mean dedicated or set apart for certain purposes, like how some people keep a pair of shoes for special occasions. In certain contexts, it may describe a follower of Christ being distinct from the world by conduct and speech. It can also mean "pure" or "without stain." This last meaning best fits the context of the passages above.

Unlike passages that call on believers to be holy, these passages tell us that God made us holy in Christ. The cross lifted our moral stains and cleansed us of all our guilt. This allows God to see us as completely innocent in our new identity.

Years ago, I watched a movie called *The Truman Show*. It's a sci-fi comedy about the life of an upbeat 30-year-old named Truman Burbank. But the opening scene reveals Truman's life is far from ordinary. Truman's hometown is actually a movie set inside an enormous dome, equipped with thousands of hidden cameras. The show broadcasts his life 24 hours a day. All the people he knows are actors. Truman has no clue that he has been the star of a reality TV show since birth.

Likewise, the all-knowing God of the universe sees everything we've ever done and will do. Nothing escapes his notice.

On one hand, it's relieving that someone can know everything about us and still choose to love us. On the other, it's terrifying. The things we do in secret are on full display before God.

God not only knows all the things we do but also possesses exhaustive knowledge of our inner thoughts. It's often difficult to discern other people's motives, much less our own. Take any act of service. Let's say compassion moves you to join a service project serving the poor in your city. It would be difficult to claim that no mixed motives were baked into this act of kindness. Yet God has no problem parsing our thoughts and motives. "Even from far away," David admits to God, "you understand my motives" (Psalm 139:2).

On a theological level, we understand God knows everything about us. We know he can read our thoughts. And yet, we live as if he can't. We act as if what we do in secret remains hidden.

That's what makes this identity truth so astounding: Despite God's knowledge of our sin, he declares us "holy and blameless in his sight." Instead of turning away in dismay, God scrubbed us clean through the precious blood of his son, Jesus.

DEEMED NEVER TO HAVE OCCURRED

Recently, I was reviewing our application for volunteers serving in our student ministries. We require everyone to fill out a form and undergo a thorough background check before working with minors. It occurred to me that the application would probably flag me.

I spent half my teenage life in jail. I grew up in Chicago during the '90s, a period of rampant gang culture and violence. That lifestyle sucked me in like a vortex. Shortly after joining a gang, I was arrested for armed robbery and spent nearly two years in an Illinois juvenile correctional facility. Upon my release, my parents relocated me to Columbus, Ohio. They thought this would keep me away from trouble. They clearly underestimated my ability to find it. A year after moving to Columbus, I found myself in the back of a police cruiser — this time charged with aggravated assault. I spent another year and a half in a juvenile facility, where I eventually met Christ.

I assumed the courts would seal my record after I turned 21, but I called the clerk to make sure. She looked up my name and said, "I'm still seeing something here."

I didn't care if people could see my record and discover my past. Clearly, I'm open about how God changed my life. I just didn't want our staff to make an exception for me because of my role in the church.

So, I applied to get my record expunged. The juvenile prosecutor's office was required to object due to the nature of the crime. They scheduled a hearing for me to appeal before a magistrate.

The hearing took all of 10 minutes. I explained to the magistrate how my relationship with Jesus utterly changed my life and that God used my spiritual community as a powerful catalyst for that change. I pointed out that I haven't had a run in with the police for 25 years and haven't even gotten a speeding ticket in 15.

"This process has forced me to reexamine my past," I told the magistrate.

"My life is so different now. It's as if I'm looking at a different person's life."

The magistrate turned to the prosecutor: "Counsel, is it true that he hasn't had a traffic ticket in 15 years?"

"As far as the investigator can tell, Your Honor, yes," the prosecutor said. He then addressed me: "In that case, I grant your expungement."

He continued, "In all my years, this is one of the most successful stories I've ever heard. I hope you share your story and continue to inspire people with it."

A month passed before I received a letter in the mail. I grabbed it as my family and I were rushing out of the house. My wife read it to me as I drove. Most of the jargon was meaningless to anyone without a law degree. But the last line caught my attention:

> [THE COURT ORDERS] THE RECORD BE EXPUNGED AND THAT THE PROCEEDINGS IN THE CASE BE DEEMED NEVER TO HAVE OCCURRED.

Until that moment, this whole process felt like a formality. But when my wife read that line, I realized it was symbolic of how God views me and my sin. The moment I asked God to forgive me through Jesus, he deemed all the things I had ever done wrong as if they never occurred.

FREE FROM ACCUSATION

God washed us clean of our moral guilt with Jesus' blood, which allows us to live "free from accusation" (Colossians 1:22). Even so, God's enemy, Satan, probes for weaknesses. Once he identifies an insecurity or a character defect, he exploits it by convincing you that you are your biggest flaw. Or he seizes an opening — right after you fall into sin — to pour on the accusations. He wants you to define yourself by your worst mistakes. He wants you to believe that who you are at your worst is who you really are.

If you try to follow Jesus in a serious way, you will face a barrage of accusations from God's enemy. You will hear thoughts like these whispered in your ear:

Don't let people get too close. Once they find out about your past, they will never look at you the same.

Once people get to know you, you will be exposed for what you really are.

You think you can just waltz into God's presence? Why would God answer any of your prayers after what you've done?

Why are you acting like you're committed to God when you still have lingering doubts? Who are you fooling? You're a fraud.

Our new identity in Christ neutralizes this threat. We are holy in God's sight, without blemish and free from accusation. People are free to think what they want, but that does not change what God thinks. The only opinion that matters is his, and God declares that he blotted out your morally stained past.

Jesus' death frees us from lingering regret as well. Years ago, I was talking to a friend struggling with discouragement about his life and ministry. As we tried to figure out why he was feeling this way, he told me about an incident that happened years earlier. He had embezzled money from his roommates. Over time, the Spirit's prompting led him to confess. He told me, "Not a day goes by when I don't think about what I've done." I reminded him that repentance leaves no room for regret, because God has washed us clean by the blood of Jesus.

Regret, shame, guilt and accusations will at times enter your mind. You must counter these thoughts with what Scripture says. You must stand firm on the truth by presenting yourself to God in your new identity.

Merciful Father, it boggles my mind to think that you blot out my morally stained past and remember my sins no more. Thank you so much that you unburdened me of the guilt that continuously weighed me down. Help me avoid the snare of self-righteousness by reminding me that you wiped my slate clean and view me as morally pure and without any blemishes in Christ. I pray this in the name of your son, Jesus. Amen.

TWO
Sealed with the Spirit

You also were included in Christ when you heard the message
of truth, the gospel of your salvation. When you believed, you
were marked in him with a seal, the promised Holy Spirit, who
is a deposit guaranteeing our inheritance until the redemption of
those who are God's possession — to the praise of his glory.
EPHESIANS 1:13-14

Now the one who has fashioned us for this very purpose is
God, who has given us the Spirit as a deposit, guaranteeing
what is to come.
2 CORINTHIANS 5:5

Placing our trust in Christ sealed our destiny. It guaranteed our salvation. Nothing in all of creation will ever be able to separate us from God's love (Romans 8:39). God certifies this by giving us the Holy Spirit. Above, the Apostle Paul uses two different metaphors to describe this process.

First, he tells us God marked us with his seal when he gave us the Holy Spirit. In the ancient world, a king would send a courier to deliver a letter. The king would either fold the letter or roll it into a scroll. He would drip hot wax onto the seams and press his signet ring with the engraved royal seal into the wax. This authenticated the process. The royal seal provided two things: safe travel for the courier and assurance for the recipient that no one tampered with the contents of the letter. Paul utilizes this vivid image to describe God sealing us with his Spirit.

Paul also tells us that the Spirit acts as a deposit guaranteeing our inheritance. Modern Greek uses this word for an engagement ring. In the ancient world, people used it to describe a down payment for large purchases.

We still practice this today. If someone decides to buy a house, the seller asks for earnest money. This token amount — one to three percent of the sale price — assures the seller you're serious about purchasing the house. If you back out, the seller keeps the money.

Likewise, God gave us a guarantee of our future inheritance. The Holy Spirit represents the first installment of what he will give us in the next life. That means the indwelling Spirit of God is a foretaste and promise of what is to come.

It's hard to exaggerate the role God's Spirit plays in our lives. The Spirit is the primary conduit through which God interacts with us. The Holy Spirit's activity is proof of God's love for us. And it provides security in our relationship with him.

SECURITY IN OUR SALVATION

Many believers spend their time in prayer shaking their clasped hands toward heaven, asking God not to reject them. This should not be the tone of our time with God. We bear the seal of God's Spirit, which ensures our entry into heaven. Consider a few more passages that speak to our assurance of salvation.

Romans 8:1 There is now no condemnation for those who are in Christ Jesus.

1 John 4:18 There is no fear in love. But perfect love drives out fear, because fear has to do with punishment. The one who fears is not made perfect in love.

John 10:27-29 "My sheep listen to my voice; I know them, and they follow me. I give them eternal life, and they shall never perish; no one will snatch them out of my hand. My Father, who has given them to me, is greater than all; no one can snatch them out of my Father's hand."

How should our eternal security change the way we approach God? Instead of cowering or beating our chests in regret, we can come to him with full assurance of his acceptance. Thanksgiving, praise and openness should fill our time with God — not fear, anxiety and guardedness. The security of God's seal drives our focus outward, laboring in prayer for those we love and serve.

The tone of our time with God also impacts our faithfulness. Fear that arises from threats compels us to do what it takes to appease; whereas gratitude that emerges from grace inspires us to do what will please. Do we view God as a wrath-filled tyrant to placate? Or do we view him like a loving Father whom we obey with gladness?

PROOF OF GOD'S LOVE

God gives the Holy Spirit to affirm his love for us. "God's love has been poured out into our hearts through the Holy Spirit" as evidence of God's steadfast commitment to us (Romans 5:5). The Spirit shows us God's love in various ways.

Provides Comfort

Trials, hardships and suffering can disrupt joy. The sadness and grief we feel during these times can overwhelm us. Heartache may create doubt about God's goodness.

God does not show indifference to our suffering. Scripture declares God to be "the Father of compassion and the God of all comfort" (2 Corinthians 1:3). He comforts us in all our troubles.

How does God offer us comfort? Jesus gives us the answer, "I will ask the Father, and He will give you another Comforter, that He may be with you forever" (John 14:16). God doesn't just send people to comfort us in times of distress. He offers us inner peace, encouragement and hope through his comforter, the Holy Spirit.

God's Spirit directs our attention toward God's promises amid suffering, calling to mind relevant Scripture. He will prompt us to share about our suffering with a sympathetic ear. The Spirit even speaks on our behalf when emotions short-circuit our ability to express thoughts to God. Paul tells us that "the Spirit also helps our weakness; for we do not know how to pray as we should, but the Spirit Himself intercedes for *us* with groanings too deep for words" (Romans 8:26, NASB).

Gives Guidance and Wisdom

Matthew gives us the following observation when Jesus saw the throng of sick and desperate people, "When he saw the crowds, he had compassion on them because they were bewildered and helpless, like sheep without a shepherd" (Matthew 9:36). We often walk around confused and helpless. We put on masks of self-assurance and happiness. We pretend as if we have life figured out.

Life creates anxiety. So we absorb ourselves with projects at work, we occupy our minds with various life goals, and we obsess over hobbies. And yet, confusion blows into our minds like a stormfront in quiet moments.

The Spirit gives us wisdom and direction, just as a lamp illuminates our path at night. Jesus told his followers that when the Holy Spirit comes, "He will guide you into all the truth" (John 16:13). Even when the meaning of a specific situation may remain hidden from us, God's purpose is not. He discloses his intention to use all the situations we face in life for our good (Romans 8:28).

The Spirit also directs our path day to day. Paul reminds us in Galatians 5:25, "Since we live by the Spirit, let us keep in step with the Spirit." The Spirit of God offers guidance as we make major life decisions and as we consider how to spur others toward loving God and people.

Illuminates Our Thinking

Without the Spirit, the meaning of spiritual truths lies just out of reach. We can grasp concepts in Scripture, yet they contain no significance for our life. Look at this description of spiritual blindness:

> The person without the Spirit does not accept the things that come from the Spirit of God but considers them foolishness and cannot understand them because they are discerned only through the Spirit. (1 Corinthians 2:14)

We cannot reason our way to God. We need revelation. The Fall — mankind's original rebellion from God — distorted our minds and corrupted our will. It displaced God from the primary position in our life and replaced him with our affections and desires set on overdrive.

When the Spirit enters our life, he illuminates our thinking as electricity ignites the filament in a lightbulb. In the same passage describing our state of spiritual blindness, God tells us what happens when the Spirit instructs our mind with the truth.

> What we have received is… the Spirit who is from God, so that we may understand what God has freely given us. This is what we speak, not in words taught us by human wisdom but in words taught by the Spirit, explaining spiritual realities with Spirit-taught words. (1 Corinthians 2:12-13)

Evidence for God's existence keeps my faith fixed to a firm foundation. It gives me confidence that my beliefs are established in objective reality. Seeing the Spirit transform someone's life gives me subjective evidence of this reality.

I've met many brilliant believers who, prior to receiving Christ, came off as obtuse while discussing spiritual matters. They seemed to have trouble wrapping their minds around the meaning of the gospel — even after hearing it dozens of times. Then one day, their spiritual understanding swelled as if someone opened a floodgate. They started sharing spiritual insights from Scripture. It was clear that God enlightened their understanding through the illuminating work of the Holy Spirit. God uses this explosion of insight to prove the reality of his presence to the new believer.

Transforms Us To Become More Like Jesus

Over the course of your Christian life, God will uncover problem areas that you want to change, or he will shine a spotlight on sin that's hurting people around you. Out of desperation, you may plead with God for help: *Lord, help me to be more patient with my wife and kids. Father, help me break my alcohol addiction. God, give me the fortitude to resist sexual immorality with my girlfriend.*

God will give you steps to be more patient or a way out of temptation. But he also gives you the Spirit who bears fruit in your life in the form of character change. Galatians 5:22-23 says, "The fruit of the Spirit is love, joy, peace, patience, kindness, goodness, faithfulness, gentleness, self-control." Jesus displayed all these character qualities during his life on earth. And God desires nothing short of Christ-like character for you. He is committed to carrying out this work until you see Jesus face to face and become like him.

Fills Us with Satisfaction

Much of the grief and sadness in life comes from the emptiness we feel inside. God designed us with a spiritual dimension so that we could be connected to him. But we were born into a fallen world, damaged and fragmented. That's why no matter what we do, how much we consume, or who we are with, we are never satisfied. Something is still missing. Scripture teaches that only God's presence will make us whole. At the height of Jesus' ministry, he stood up before the crowds and cried out:

> "If any man is thirsty, let him come to Me and drink. He who believes in Me, as the Scripture said, 'From his innermost being shall flow rivers of living water.'" He [was speaking] of the Spirit, those who believed in Him were to receive. (John 7:37-39)

God quenches our inner thirst by pouring the Holy Spirit into our hearts. He fills us with his boundless love — offering us the fulfillment and inner peace we can find nowhere else.

Lord, I praise you that you are generous. I thank you for all the good things you have given us in Christ. I'm especially grateful that you gave us the promised Holy Spirit, who is not only with us but also indwells us. Let the assurance and security you offer us through the Spirit alter the way we approach you. Let it shape the way we interact with you. Let it change the way we live for you. In your son's name we pray, Amen.

THREE
New Creation in Christ

So from now on we regard no one from a worldly point of view. Though we once regarded Christ in this way, we do so no longer. Therefore, if anyone is in Christ, the new creation has come: The old has gone, the new is here!
2 CORINTHIANS 5:16-17

God hit the reset button on our lives when we received Jesus. We became new people in his eyes, reborn into a life that will stretch into eternity. This fact impacts us along two dimensions. Vertically, we have a new standing before God that shapes the way we relate to him. Horizontally, we start to see other followers of Christ as they are in him. Let's explore these two areas in more detail.

VERTICALLY

The biblical understanding of human nature stands in stark contrast to other worldviews. Scripture teaches that we enter this world morally corrupt, separated and alienated from God. Our estrangement continues to grow as we rebel against him.

To make matters worse, the Lord demands moral perfection since he is morally perfect. His righteous character demands punishment for wrongs we've committed.

Yet, Scripture also reveals that God is merciful. He chose to show us mercy instead of giving us what we deserve. "While we were God's enemies," Paul explains, "we were reconciled to him through the death of his Son" (Romans 5:10). God the Father's compassion drove him to send Jesus to pay our moral debt. By his death, Jesus restored our relationship with God. He settled our differences through the cross.

Therefore, God looks at us differently the moment we receive Christ. Our heavenly Father adopts us as heirs to his kingdom. He no longer regards us as his enemies, we are his children. More than this, the Apostle Paul declares that God chose us before the creation of the world so that we might be "holy and blameless in his sight" (Ephesians 1:4).

Jesus faced all the temptation we do, yet he never fell into sin (Hebrews 4:15). He lived a morally perfect life. Therefore, when God gives us a new identity in Christ, he clears us of all our guilt. We literally take on Christ's attributes: "God made him who had no sin to be sin for us, so that in him we might become the righteousness of God" (2 Corinthians 5:21).

What he sees and what we see in the mirror may differ. We see all our flaws, all our problems and all our past mistakes. How is it possible to view ourselves as God's new creation? The Apostle Paul supplies us with a vivid mental picture, "For all of you who were baptized into Christ have clothed yourselves with Christ" (Galatians 3:27). The image of putting on bright, new, clean clothing fits with Paul's joyous exclamation that, in Christ, "the old has gone, the new is here!" (2 Corinthians 5:17).

The Old Has Gone

God no longer sees who we were or what we did before we met Christ. From his point of view, that person is gone. We died when Jesus died. Who God says we are now, defines who we are. That's why Paul was able to say, "From now on we recognize no one according to the flesh... if anyone is in Christ, he is a new creature" (2 Corinthians 5:16).

Often feelings of guilt haunt us from our past. We've hurt people or taken things from people. We've caused permanent damage to people's lives, destroyed relationships or betrayed those we love. For some of us, guilt runs so deep we think about it almost every day.

Guilt is the enemy of grace. It forces us to fix our eyes on what we have done wrong. It produces a counterfeit motive to live for God based on works. Ultimately, it blocks us from drawing near to him and receiving his mercy.

You shouldn't mistake guilt for godly conviction. God can put things on our hearts to own, admit and change. But bearing the burden of guilt doesn't fit our new standing in Christ. Who we were and what we've done are gone. But here's the problem: How God sees us and how we see ourselves are often different.

Are you are still holding on to feelings of guilt from your past? If so, you are living in a way that doesn't line up with God's perspective. And his perception of the world is reality. If God declares you blameless in Christ, then you are indeed.

If you are carrying the weight of guilt and shame, turn to God and express how you are feeling. Tell him that you know what Scripture says about your standing in Christ, but that you're having a hard time believing it. Keep presenting yourself to God as a new creation in Christ, and over time your guilt will subside (Romans 6:13). Over time, your feelings will conform to the truth. And you can unburden yourself of the guilt you've been carrying like removing a heavy backpack after a long trip.

The New Is Here

Can you imagine what life would look like if we never felt shame? Shame, whether imagined or real, creates distance in our relationships. We often misread situations. A friend didn't hear us say hello at a party.

We interpret this as her ignoring us. Your mother snaps at you during a holiday gathering. This confirms your worst suspicion that you're a disappointment to the family.

We experience the same with God. Feelings of shame and guilt often accompany moral failure. The last thing we want to do is turn to God after falling into sin. We feel as if God is disappointed with us, so we avoid him.

God isn't angry at you. In his perfect knowledge of the future, he saw you falling into sin and made a payment on your behalf 2,000 years ago. Jesus paid for all the sins you have committed — and will commit — throughout your life. This explains why he can regard you as holy and blameless in his sight.

Maybe you have recently experienced moral failure. You're struggling to see yourself as God sees you. You're racked with feelings of guilt. Realize this: Your feelings of guilt are just that — feelings. God cleared you of your guilt in Christ. Therefore, put your faith in what God says about your new identity and present yourself to him with confidence. He eagerly awaits your restoration and transformation. But he's waiting for you to take the first step.

HORIZONTALLY

Our new identity should not only alter how we relate to God; it should change how we relate to other believers. Grasping our new identity means seeing ourselves the way God sees us and seeing others the way God sees them.

Let's be honest. Sometimes people in our spiritual community irritate us. Some members argue as if it's a competitive sport. They like to take the contrary view, even if they don't believe it. Then you have your know-it-alls. They're experts in every subject. You can't forget the compulsive talker. You brace yourself for the verbal tsunami that comes whenever she opens her mouth. Finally, you have your self-absorbed person. He always finds a way to shift the focus back to him.

Of course, we are experts at seeing other people's problems and not our own. Ironically, we tend to reserve our harshest judgment for those who share the same problems. We can see right through their excuses or their thinly veiled attempts to conceal sin because we use the same tactics. We all must admit that we have problems. Each of us contributes to the messiness of life in God's community.

More than anyone, God sees our struggles. Our character defects lay bare before his omniscience. This forced King David to confess, "God, you know how foolish I am; my sins cannot be hidden from you" (Psalm 69:5). God sees every single thing wrong with us.

Yet, he doesn't write us off. He doesn't see us as a source of irritation he must tolerate. He doesn't hold a negative view of us. Instead, he refuses to identify us by our moral failure. He recreates us in Christ. He imparts a new identity and declares us holy and blameless in his sight.

Renaissance artist Michelangelo was renowned for his breathtaking sculptures, completing his two most famous pieces, *La Pietà* and *David*, before age 30. Many art historians observe the balance of composition in his sculptures. Michelangelo was able to arrange his figures in expressive poses while maintaining a simple structure.

When someone asked how he was able to achieve this balance, Michelangelo famously said that he imagined his figures trapped inside the marble slab. He saw his task as removing the material that encased them. Michelangelo was able to see the potential in every raw piece of marble he chose.

Likewise, God views every believer in Christ as his masterpiece. He sees the potential in every one of his followers, no matter how annoying or frustrating they may be. He sees beyond their problems, their relational glitches and their sin habits. He looks past all of these and sees who they are in Christ. Paul exclaims, "For we are God's masterpiece. He has created us anew in Christ Jesus, so we can do the good things he planned for us long ago" (Ephesians 2:10).

How about you? Do you have a vision for what God will do in the lives of people around you? Do you see how God may use you to play a part in transforming them? Or do you see fellow believers as a nuisance? God wants you to see past their problems and discover their potential in Christ.

If the all-powerful God commits himself to chipping away the imperfections in a believer's life, then you shouldn't wave off that person in contempt. Instead, you should show them the same kind of care and love God shows them.

Father, it's difficult to see ourselves and others as we are in Christ. I pray that you would take this abstract concept and make it a reality for us. Let our new identity in Christ shape the way we approach you and the way we treat fellow believers. Help us to see people as they are in Christ. Amen.

FOUR
Free from the Law

It is for freedom that Christ has set us free. Stand firm, then, and do not let yourselves be burdened again by a yoke of slavery.
GALATIANS 5:1

So, my brothers and sisters, you also died to the law through the body of Christ, that you might belong to another, to him who was raised from the dead, in order that we might bear fruit for God.
ROMANS 7:4

Have you ever tried to read the Bible cover to cover? You hit a wall when you read the first five books because they contain 613 commands. This is what the New Testament refers to as "the Law." The Law is a mixture of ritual rules, moral regulations and civil ordinances for the nation of Israel.

So, what purpose does the Law serve for believers? If you are a follower of Jesus, then you are no longer under its rule. God sent his son Jesus, "born under the law, to redeem those under the law" (Galatians 4:4). This means we don't have to fulfill the demands of the Law because Jesus fulfilled them for us. We died to the Law because Jesus died for us.

So, what now? Do we just discard 20 percent of the Bible? Is it completely irrelevant? Before we answer these questions, let's try to wrap our minds around what the Lord intended to do through the Law.

WHAT DOES GOD HOPE TO ACCOMPLISH?

First, the law defines sin. The Bible teaches that if God did not reveal his moral will, we would be hopeless to figure it out. The Fall damaged the calibration of our moral compass. Therefore, we have a difficult time knowing right from wrong. We need a standard by which to judge our attitudes and actions.

Imagine growing up in rural Indiana during the early 1960s. Basketball is the most popular sport in your town. From a young age, people have made comments about your talent as a player. By your senior year, everyone regards you as the best in town. You average 30 points per game with a 40 percent shooting average. You tower over most people at six foot four inches tall. You conclude that you are one of the best basketball players on the planet.

What you don't know is that there is a man named Wilt Chamberlain. He stands more than seven feet tall and scored 100 points in a single NBA game before the three-point line existed. His shooting percentage is more than 50 percent.

You were determining your skill level based on comparisons drawn from other players in your small town. You did not have an external, objective standard by which you could judge if you are great.

Likewise, we often determine if we are a good person based on comparisons to the people around us. Yet, that's not an objective standard to judge what God deems good enough.

This partly explains why God gave us the Law. It presents a dim reflection of God's perfect moral character. Just as the best player in the NBA provides a standard to measure others, God provides the Law to give us a standard that can judge our attitudes and actions.

Second, the Law provokes us to sin. This may seem strange, even contradictory to some. Romans 5:20 assures us that "the law came in so that the transgression may increase, but where sin increased, grace multiplied all the more." God did not give us the Law to prevent sin. He gave it so that sin "may increase."

Last fall, my family and I traveled to Acadia National Park in Maine. During our vacation we hiked around Jordan Pond, a popular path in the park. Along the trail, we saw an odd-looking tree. It was three feet tall with a single large branch jutting out the side. It looked as if someone attached a capital "J" to a stump. The bark on the curved area of the branch was smooth and well-worn.

My kids and I walked over to get a closer look. The National Park Service had placed a wooden inlay on the branch that said, "Do not sit on tree." I blinked, and my kids were sitting and climbing on the branch. I guess if you want to create curiosity or excitement around something, forbid it.

You might say, "In that case, then maybe there's something wrong with the Law." There's nothing wrong with the Law; there's something wrong with us. Our instinct is do the opposite of what God says. When our sin nature contacts God's commands, it incites us to rebel. Thus, the Law only exposes the enormity and depth of our problem — it doesn't cause it.

Finally, the Law leads us to Christ. Galatians 3:24 insists, "the Law has become our tutor to lead us to Christ, so that we may be justified by faith." The Law points us to Christ by showing us the magnitude of our sin and the magnificence of his sacrifice. The unbearable weight of God's demands forces us to decide: Pretend you are righteous, or admit you are a sinner. The latter puts us one step closer to throwing ourselves on God's mercy and receiving Christ.

WHAT ROLE DOES THE LAW HAVE IN OUR LIVES?

Scripture offers us an unequivocal answer: We are no longer under the Law. In his seminal chapter, Paul reminds believers, "My brothers and sisters, you also died to the law through the body of Christ" (Romans 7:4). In another place he says, "For through the law I died to the law so that I might live for God" (Galatians 2:19).

Many Christian authors argue, however, that these passages refer to a believer's salvation. They would argue the Law still plays a useful role in spiritual growth. Yet both verses above apply to spiritual growth. Paul fires a string of rhetorical questions at the Galatian believers who thought they needed to go back under Law after receiving Jesus:

> I would like to learn just one thing from you: Did you receive the Spirit by the works of the law, or by believing what you heard? Are you so foolish? After beginning by means of the Spirit, are you now trying to finish by means of the flesh? (Galatians 3:2-3)

He was criticizing these believers because they were trying to reach spiritual maturity through the Law. God makes it clear that we attain spiritual growth in the same way we receive salvation: It's by faith, not through works. Romans 1:17 reminds us:

> This Good News tells us how God makes us right in his sight. This is accomplished from start to finish by faith. As the Scriptures say, "The righteous will live by faith."

God wouldn't offer us salvation by grace through faith, then switch it up by saying we need to grow through the works of the Law.

However, this doesn't mean that we should discard the Law. Scripture tells us that God the Father wants us to become more like his son, Jesus. That's at the heart of spiritual growth. The Law, then, gives us a standard of Christ-likeness since it's a dim picture of God's perfect moral character. And we can measure our progress by how much we love others, "For whoever loves others has fulfilled the law" (Romans 13:8).

Getting out from under the Law to grow presumes that God does the heavy lifting to transform our character. Only his mighty hand can produce lasting change. Yet we play a crucial role, too. God calls on us to participate in the process by immersing ourselves in his word, engaging in prayer, taking steps of faith to serve and surrounding ourselves in Christian community.

Of course, our fallen human nature resists depending on God. We revert to a works-based relationship with God, what Scripture calls being "under the Law." This shift is so subtle that we often do not notice until our walks start to break down.

SYMPTOMS THAT YOU ARE UNDER THE LAW

One sign of living under the law is bitter envy, a corrosive resentment toward those who have what you want. You are stunned by their prosperity, and you take perverse delight in their adversity. Author and theologian Cornelius Plantinga gives us an insightful picture of envy's effects:

> Envious people backbite. They deliver congratulations with a smile that, in another light, might be taken for a sneer. They acknowledge someone's praise of a rival but then push their rival into the shadow of a master... The envier gossips. He saves up bad news of others and passes it around like an appetizer at happy hour. The envier grumbles. He murmurs. He complains that all the wrong people are getting ahead.[5]

Sometimes bitter envy aimed at others morphs into anger toward God. Asaph, an author of many psalms, complains to God, "Surely in vain I have kept my heart pure and washed my hands in innocence" (Psalm 73:13). Asaph looks around and sees those who disregard God living trouble-free lives while he faces trials and hardship. He envies the ease of his enemies. This causes him to lash out against God. He nearly loses his faith. He confesses, "My feet had almost slipped; I had nearly lost my foothold. For I envied the arrogant when I saw the prosperity of the wicked" (Psalm 73:2-3).

This is the trap of living under the Law. If you think that living for God entitles you to a smooth path in life, then anger will consume you, since life never turns out as you expect. You will feel you deserve better than you get. You will grow to resent people because of their success or, conversely, for their lack of hardship. Your resentment, however, is your own fault. It has nothing to do with the success of others, but comes from your insistence that God owes you a good life after all you have done for him.[6]

At other times, being under the Law expresses itself in a strong sense of superiority. Those trapped in this mindset take their identity from their hard work, moral fortitude or membership in an exclusive group. They compare themselves with others to establish their sense of self-worth. When you look at the world through this lens, it becomes easy to look at others with an air of superiority and hyper-criticism. Christian author and professor of church history Richard Lovelace captures this well:

> [People] who are no longer sure that God loves and accepts them in Jesus, apart from their present spiritual achievements, are subconsciously radically insecure persons… Their insecurity shows itself in pride, a fierce, defensive assertion of their own righteousness, and defensive criticism of others. They come naturally to hate other cultural styles… in order to bolster their own security and discharge their suppressed anger.[7]

Burnout is another sign that you are buckling under the load of the Law. If you do God's work God's way, you will have stamina to go the distance. If you try to do it through human effort, you will wear down. An older Christian once said to me, "You should feel tired *from* doing God's work, but you should never grow tired *of* doing God's work." That's an indicator of burnout. If you are not drawing from the infinite reserves of God's power, you are attempting to fulfill his commands without his power. That's the essence of living under the Law.

FAILING TO LIVE UP TO THE LAW

As followers of Jesus, we fluctuate between living under the Law and under grace. We desire to become more like Jesus, but we try to attain this through our own effort. We make progress in our spiritual growth, but we forget that God's power brought the change. We see success serving God, but we credit it to our own cleverness or charisma.

I recently went to a park near downtown Columbus that has an elaborate obstacle course with a tunnel crawl, a cargo net climb and tire flip. You can push small car tires or enormous tractor tires. I watched as children tried to complete the course. Without fail, each one ran past the smaller ones meant for them and toward the giant tractor tires. They would squat down and try to lift the hulking donut with all their might, their bodies trembling. But the tire sat still, undisturbed.

In the same way, God watches as we strain to meet the demands of the Law. He knows we can't bear its weight. He's waiting for us to admit defeat.

The Lord doesn't allow us to fail because he takes pleasure in our distress. He knows that when we fail, we're one step away from experiencing victory. Look at how Paul struggled in this area:

> I do not understand what I do. For what I want to do I do not do, but what I hate I do. And if I do what I do not want to do, I agree that the law is good. As it is, it is no longer I myself who do it, but it is sin living in me… For I have the desire to do what is good, but I cannot carry it out. For I do not do the good I want to do, but the evil I do not want to do — this I keep on doing. (Romans 7:15-19)

Every follower of Jesus can relate. We feel this internal struggle. Part of us wants to do good. The other part of us, our sin nature, wants the opposite. It draws us toward the very thing we do not want to do. Paul vents his frustration to the Roman believers as he reaches a point of despair: "Wretched man I am! Who will rescue me from this body that is subject to death?" (7:24). Paul seems to be having a crisis of faith. But his cry of despair ends in a note of victory: "Thanks be to God, who delivers me through Jesus Christ our Lord" (7:25).

As my close friend, Dennis McCallum, once said, "Dependence on Jesus begins at precisely the point where dependence on self ends."[8]

Father, I am grateful that I'm no longer under the Law for spiritual growth. Thank you that your son fulfilled it on my behalf. I pray that you show me when I am falling into legalistic thinking and help me to come under your grace. Amen.

FIVE
No Longer Slaves to Sin

Knowing this, that our old self was crucified with Him, in order
that our body of sin might be done away with, so that we would
no longer be slaves to sin.

ROMANS 6:6

Thanks be to God that, though you used to be slaves to sin,
you have come to obey from your heart the pattern of teaching
that has now claimed your allegiance. You have been set free
from sin and have become slaves to righteousness.

ROMANS 6:17-18

"Everyone who sins is a slave to sin," Jesus declared (John 8:34). Each of us has experienced these enslaving effects. We've all felt the attractional force of temptation. We can recall times when we've hung our heads in shame after succumbing to a burning desire. We've all despaired over the inability to break a bad pattern.

James vividly describes this lifecycle: "Each person is tempted when they are dragged away by their own evil desire and enticed. Then, after desire has conceived, it gives birth to sin; and sin, when it is full-grown, gives birth to death" (James 1:14-15). The more we give in, the more of our humanity we forfeit. Sin robs us of freedom. It changes us into the worst versions of ourselves.

The driving force behind our enslavement to sin is rebellion. The Apostle Paul details the stairstep descent of sin as he warns the Ephesians about returning to their old way of life before meeting Christ:

> You must no longer live as the Gentiles do, in the futility of their thinking. They are darkened in their understanding and separated from the life of God because of the ignorance that is in them due to the hardening of their hearts. Having lost all sensitivity, they have given themselves over to sensuality so as to indulge in every kind of impurity, and they are full of greed. (Ephesians 4:17-19)

Living in the "futility" of our mind describes man's attempt to make sense of the world without God. Paul says that living in the futility of our mind is the first step in the descent of sin. Such an approach results in a hardened heart toward God. In turn, this darkens understanding and dulls spiritual sensitivity. Having lost this, we give ourselves over to pleasure, comfort and pulsating desires. Our appetite eventually places its foot on our neck.

LOSS OF FREEDOM

Modern Western man places ultimate value on freedom. As theologian Tim Keller puts it, "Modern people view giving individuals freedom as the main role of any institution and of society itself. This has always been important in our society, but now it is ultimately important."[9] Modern people view freedom as a form of self-assertion. *I'm free; therefore, I can do whatever I want.*[10]

Yet, unbounded, undirected liberty doesn't result in true freedom. It leads to enslavement. When you experience the pleasure of getting high or sexual release, you find yourself desiring that same feeling of euphoria and arousal. So naturally, you seek out another experience. But you notice that the high or sexual release doesn't feel quite as good as the first time. So, you increase the amount of drugs you take or multiply sexual encounters. At first, this gets you close; over time, it just gets you back to normal.

In the end, you may find yourself hopelessly addicted to drugs or sexual experiences. You find yourself doing things that you never thought you would do just to get back that high or feeling of release. You see, giving yourselves over to what the Bible defines as sin isn't an expression of freedom; it's the road to slavery.

Some of you might say, "I don't do drugs. I don't drink. I don't sleep around." But the same thing applies to bad relational habits. For instance, if at a young age you discover that bending the truth can help you avoid embarrassing situations or negative consequences, you may pursue lying as a strategy for escaping trouble. Years of distorting and concealing the truth hardens into a habit of compulsive lying. Over time, you may lose the ability tell what's even true.

You could also apply this to selfishness. If you put self at the center, people around you feel the burden of your love demands. You lose the ability to see other people's perspectives when you disagree with them. Over the years, selfishness can mutate into self-absorption and, worse, narcissism. Once these tendencies take hold, it's difficult to break free.

I WILL NEVER CHANGE

Some people's struggles are so engrained, they construct an identity from them. For some, it's an addiction. They tell themselves and others, "I am an alcoholic," or "I am a sex addict." Others scold themselves, "I keep falling into sin. I'll never change." Yet, this contradicts what Paul declares about our new identity in Romans 6: "We're no longer slaves to sin." The moment we came to Christ, we left our old identity at the cross, for "our old self was crucified with Him" (Romans 6:6).

Unfortunately, many Christians live in ignorance of this fact and remain enslaved to sin.

In 1863, Abraham Lincoln signed an executive order called the Emancipation Proclamation. This declared all the slaves in the southern states free. What effect do you think this had on the slaves in the South? None at first. I doubt many plantation owners rushed to the bunkhouses clutching a newspaper, eager to share the good news with their slaves. Indeed, firsthand accounts survive of slaves who continued to work the fields months or in some cases years after the signed order.[11] Their legal identity changed the moment Lincoln inked the executive order; yet they didn't know it. They continued living as slaves even though they were free.[12] Likewise, many Christians believe they're enslaved to a pattern of sin.

The fact is, our new standing in Christ has liberated us from sin's control. Our new identity has robbed sin's power over us, just as the Emancipation Proclamation robbed owners of legal claim to their slaves.

FACTS VS. FEELINGS

Simply filing facts into your mind about your new identity isn't enough to change your life. You will often encounter a collision between facts and feelings. Your feelings often contradict what God declares is true of you. That's why you must exert faith. You need to reject what your feelings are telling you in favor of what God says.

Let's go back to our illustration of freed slaves in the South. What difference would it make if after hearing news about their freedom, slaves went back to the fields in disbelief? Simply knowing about their freedom wasn't enough. These free men and women had to believe what they heard to benefit from their new legal standing. Tragically, many ex-slaves continued to serve their former masters after learning about their freedom. According to New York University history professor David Orshinsky:

> Among the hundreds of ex-slaves interviewed in the 1930s, about forty percent claimed to have moved during the war itself

or in the months immediately following emancipation. But most remained where they were, living as tenants or field hands on the same land they had worked all along… The exhilaration of moving was tempered by feelings of insecurity and fear.

"We wanted to be free at times, [then] we would get [scared and] want to stay slaves," a freedman recalled. "We was [told] all kinds of things but didn't know [just] what to believe."[13]

In the same way, I've met countless believers who knew about their new identity in Christ and still felt stuck. Though they knew what God said about them, they simply refused to accept it. Much like the ex-slaves quoted above, they often refuse to believe they will change or they're afraid to leave their old way of life.

COUNTING

In one of the most important passages on spiritual growth, Paul charges us, "Count yourselves dead to sin but alive to God in Christ Jesus" (Romans 6:11). People often used the word "count" as a technical term in the ancient world. It described the act of entering something into a ledger or charging something to an account.

To count something implies taking inventory of what's already there. Unlike the modern concept of "positive thinking," we are not putting our hope in something that's uncertain. When God tells us to "count" something, he's telling us to believe what's objectively true. Therefore, God isn't asking us to try and imagine "ourselves as dead to sin but alive to God in Christ Jesus." He's not telling us to pretend that we've been liberated from sin's grip on our lives. He's calling on us to see what's true about us in Christ.

And yet, we face one major obstacle: How we see ourselves. Our experience does not line up with reality because it takes time to embrace our new identity in Christ. It's difficult to break the pattern of seeing yourself a certain way. For instance, if you grew up feeling like no one cared about you, you wouldn't immediately feel loved just because you discovered God loves you.

This raises the question: How do we begin to see ourselves as we are in Christ? Like anything else in the Christian life: Faith is the key. Hebrews 11:1 offers perhaps the most explicit definition of faith in the New Testament: "Faith is the assurance of things hoped for, the conviction of things not seen." Spiritual realities exist, for which we have no material evidence. Yet it does not make them any less real. Faith enables us to make these spiritual realities true in our experience.

Today, many things come to mind when modern people hear the word "faith." Some see faith as a matter of blind optimism. You hope and believe in an outcome that's highly unlikely. Others see faith as superstitious or anti-scientific. You appeal to the supernatural whenever you can't explain something.

Biblical faith, by contrast, stands on the foundation of objective truth. Therefore, biblical faith could be described as active trust. It's the "*assurance* of things hoped for, the *conviction* of things not seen." Thus, we must place our faith in the facts of our new identity and often the feelings follow.

So how does this work? Let's not forget what we covered in the beginning of this book. We know things. We consider them as true. We present ourselves to God on the basis of faith.

For example, feelings of despair frequently flood our minds when we face temptation: *Why even resist when I always give in anyway? I'll never change.* You must counter these thoughts with what God says is true. Commit to memory verses like Romans 6:18, "You have been set free from sin and have become slaves to righteousness." That way, you can answer these feelings of despair on demand.

You also need to present yourself to God as someone who is no longer under bondage. Turn to God in these weak moments and stand in your new identity:

Lord, I feel helpless to resist temptation right now. But you say, 'that we should no longer be slaves to sin' and that I have been freed from sin taking control of my life. Help me to see reality and resist sin.

Finally, take a step of faith. James commands, "Submit yourselves, then, to God. Resist the devil, and he will flee from you" (4:7). God will not let you be tempted beyond what you can bear (1 Corinthians 10:13). Try putting up a fight instead of giving in, and you will see victory.

<hr>

Lord, I praise you for liberating us from the bondage of sin. Conform our thinking and our view of ourselves, so that our lives may reflect this reality. I pray that you would help us resist feeling fatalistic about our sin or sinking into despair when we fall. Help us to maintain a victorious attitude toward sin, since ultimately you defeated death and sin through the cross. Amen.

SIX
Forgiven

When you were dead in your transgressions and the uncircumcision of your flesh, He made you alive together with Him, having forgiven us all our transgressions, having canceled out the certificate of debt consisting of decrees against us, which was hostile to us; and He has taken it out of the way, having nailed it to the cross.
COLOSSIANS 2:13-14

Bear with each other and forgive one another if any of you has a grievance against someone. Forgive as the Lord forgave you.
COLOSSIANS 3:13

Before we meet Jesus, each of us carries a sizeable debt to God. Every act of moral wrongdoing puts us deeper in the red. Scripture tells us that we stand condemned, not just for the amount of sin we commit, but against whom we sin. Our sin offends and provokes the judgment of a righteous God. Thus, our "certificate of debt" condemns us.

It's in this state of spiritual lifelessness that God forgave us all our sins. Scripture declares that Jesus came to earth and paid our moral debt. God nails our certificate of debt to the cross the moment we place our faith in Jesus.

This fact contains many implications, and we will spend eternity pondering them. But let's zoom in on the most important aspect of the cross, forgiveness. Maybe the best illustration of forgiveness comes from Jesus' parable of the unmerciful servant.

SHOULDN'T YOU HAVE MERCY?

One day, Simon Peter asks Jesus a simple question, "How often should I forgive someone who sins against me?" (Matthew 18:21). Jesus responds with a parable. A certain king wanted to settle accounts with those who owed him money, so a man owing an enormous debt came forward. This man owed 10,000 "talents." A talent was equal to about 6,000 denarii, and one denarius was a standard day's wage in the ancient world. My son and I were studying this passage, and we calculated it would take this man 230,769 years to pay this debt.

Since this man could not pay his debt, the king places him and his family in indentured servitude. You couldn't just declare bankruptcy in the ancient world. You found ways to pay your debts. You could arrange a payment plan, or you could work off what you owed. Top dollar for an indentured servant would fetch, maybe, one talent. This man's family would not put even a tiny dent in his debt.

The man fell to his knees and pled with the king, "Please, just give me some more time. I promise I will pay you back." He knew there was no way to pay what he owed. He was groveling for mercy. Then the king does the unthinkable: "The servant's master took pity on him, canceled the debt and let him go" (Matthew 18:27).

You'd think this man's new lease on life would change him forever. Then something odd happens.

Shortly after the king released him, the forgiven man found someone who owed him 100 denarii — the modern equivalent of three month's income. He put his hands around the man's neck and demanded the man pay him back. One of the king's servants saw this and reported it to the king. The king summoned the forgiven man and threw him in prison.

This forgiven man's response contrasts with the king's. If we examine how the king responded, it gives us three keys to forgiveness.[14]

He Took Pity on Him

If you want to guard your heart from being twisted by anger, take pity on the person who wronged you. The Greek word for pity can also mean "to feel sympathy." It means you identify with the person who angered you. It means placing yourself in the other person's shoes. To have pity means you do the deliberate, internal work of reminding yourself how much you have in common. This mental exercise helps you empathize with the person who hurt you.

Your natural impulse tells you to do the opposite. You want to highlight differences between you and your perpetrator. If you want to avoid the prison of anger, however, you need to identify with that person and say, "I'm really the same."

We perpetuate bitterness by creating a caricature of the person who wronged us. Those who have paid for a caricature know the pain of sitting while an artist sketches your face. Every minute feels like an hour. You shift in your seat while waiting to see the finished product. And when the artist reveals your portrait it's like hearing a recording of your voice. Even if the artist is being nice, he exaggerates certain features. If your ears are big, he makes them even bigger. If you have a slightly large nose, he widens or elongates it. If you have a misshaped head, he makes it look like a trapezoid.

It's the same when you want to stay angry at someone. Let's say someone lied to you.

A friend asks, "Why did he lie?"

"It's because he's a liar," you say. You've reduced him to the lie he told.

Now, if you were the one who lied, and your friend asks, "Did you lie?"

You admit, "I did."

"Why?"

"I shouldn't have done it, but it's complicated." You had your reasons. You were put in an impossible situation. What were you supposed to do? There's also important background information. You grew up in a home where you felt pressure to live up to impossible expectations. Therefore, you learned that lying appeased your parents and avoided conflict.

Nobody says, "I lied because I'm just a liar." There's always context. There's nuance. You're human. Yet when others lie, they are just a liar. We caricature the offender and excuse ourselves.

Theologian Miroslav Volf says in his book, *Exclusion and Embrace*, "Forgiveness flounders when I exclude the enemy from the community of humans, and I exclude myself from the community of sinners."[15] You can only stay mad at somebody if you tell yourself, *I am superior to them.* You refuse to admit that you are capable of doing what your enemy did.

To start the forgiveness process, identify with the person who wronged you and stop viewing them as an embodiment of their sin. If a morally perfect God could lower himself to identify with us, how can we fail to identify with a fellow sinner saved by God's grace?

He Canceled His Debt

The road to forgiveness is costly. Forgiveness is the choice between making someone pay for what they have done or absorbing the cost. Either way, someone must pay.

According to Jesus' parable, the king absorbed a tremendous loss when he canceled the servant's debt. Likewise, God absorbed the penalty we deserve to pay for our moral wrongdoing. He paid the price at the cross and canceled our debt.

Thus, God puts us in an unusual position. He removes our obligation to pay our own moral debt; at the same time, he places on us an obligation to absorb the debt of others. For the follower of Jesus, forgiveness is not an option. It is not a suggestion. It is a command.

Paul reminds the Colossians of this crucial fact, "Bear with each other and forgive one another if any of you has a grievance against someone. Forgive as the Lord forgave you" (Colossians 3:13). You are obligated to forgive because a righteous and holy God forgave you.

He Let Him Go

The king released the man from his obligation. In the Old Testament, God spoke of a time when he would wipe our slates clean: "For I will forgive their wickedness and will remember their sins no more" (Jeremiah 31:34). This is an astonishing statement.

God knows everything we've ever done. The things we do in secret are on full display before him. Despite God's exhaustive knowledge of our sin, he released us from the penalty we deserved to pay.

Now, you might be wrestling with unforgiveness. You are struggling to let go of your anger. It may be a person from your past, who took advantage of you. It could be a family member, who took out their problems on you. Maybe a friend lied or betrayed your trust. Perhaps someone in your church hurt you. In any case, you must let go of your anger.

First, the offender still has power over you. You're imprisoned to your anger and resentment. It dictates your life. A man who avoids places where he may see his ex-wife or who leaves a room when someone mentions her name is still being controlled by her. Anger keeps him from certain places and conversations.

Second, resentment and anger will consume you. American theologian and author Fredrick Buechner describes this with a vivid analogy:

> Of all the [sins], anger is possibly the most fun… To smack your lips over grievances long past, to roll over your tongue the prospect of bitter confrontations still to come, to savor to the last

toothsome morsel the pain you are giving back — in many ways it is a feast fit for a king. The chief drawback is that what you are wolfing down [at this feast] is yourself.[16]

You may be mad at someone in your life, and you are in a certain amount of denial about it. Perhaps you are aware of a person whom you have not forgiven. Or maybe you have anger forming over minor irritations that may give birth to resentment. Just like the king who let the servant go, let go of the anger you feel toward that person.

TOWARD FORGIVENESS

Let me offer a few pieces of practical advice as you take steps toward forgiveness.

Don't mistake forgiveness for a feeling. It is a choice. Forgiveness is often granted long before it is felt. It's a promise not to exact payment from someone who wronged you. It's a promise not to bring up the matter to the person, others or even yourself.

Author Dan Hamilton says forgiveness "is to deal with our emotions by sending them away — by denying ourselves the dark pleasures of venting them or fondling them in our minds."[17] We exact payments from an offender with cutting remarks, avoidance or rooting for their failure. Remember: Each time we refrain from doing these, we are absorbing the cost and making a payment.

Depending on the severity of the offense, we may need to make recurring payments. At first, it will be quite difficult. If you keep this promise, however, eventually the feeling of anger subsides. You no longer seek revenge. It is critical to see that forgiveness isn't forcing yourself to deny your feelings; it's a commitment to keep a promise despite your feelings.

Seek to reconcile when possible or appropriate. In some cases, the person who hurt you isn't alive. Or you may not know your attacker or the person who took advantage of you. In other cases, the person is dangerous or abusive. In these cases, reconciliation may not be possible.

Forgiveness does not hit the reset button on trust. The person who wronged you may earn trust in small increments over time. In some cases, he may never regain the same level of trust. The speed and degree of restoration often depends on the severity of the offense.

Forgiveness leaves room to oppose or even confront the person's behavior. The person who hurt you may show a lack of repentance by hurting others. Even so, it's impossible to speak truth in love to someone you have not forgiven.

Cultivate humility. The Apostle Paul boldly called out sin in his letters with a tone of humility and love. For example, in 1 Timothy, he named evils common throughout the Roman Empire — human trafficking, sexual immorality and perjury. Yet you do not detect a hint of self-righteousness. Do you know why? He reminds us:

> Even though I was once a blasphemer and a persecutor and a violent man, I was shown mercy because I acted in ignorance and unbelief. The grace of our Lord was poured out on me abundantly, along with the faith and love that are in Christ Jesus. (1 Timothy 1:13-14)

Paul exhibited moral righteousness while maintaining contact with the grace of God. You see, as you grapple with applying grace to your own life, you learn to identify with sinners.

One of my favorite artists is Caravaggio, a 16th-century Italian painter. Art critics often comment on his dramatic use of light. His works often contain striking contrast. In *The Taking of Christ*, Caravaggio depicts the moment Judas, accompanied by Roman soldiers and a mob carrying torches, kisses Jesus and betrays him. Unlike most artists during this period, he does not depict Judas as a villain. Caravaggio paints him with an expression that suggests Judas was haunted by what would happen to Jesus. The betrayer grasps the Lord's tunic as if to convey immediate regret for what he had done.

Why didn't Caravaggio depict Judas as an evil villain, the son of perdition? The answer lies in Caravaggio's troubled past. He gained a reputation for instigating fights and dueling. Authorities arrested him several times for brawling. Caravaggio murdered a man during a duel, fled and died from illness four years later. He didn't demonize Judas because he could identify with him.

If you take a close look at the painting, you will discover the artist painted himself as one of the members of the mob seizing Jesus.

Lord, we praise you for your mercy and compassion. You had no obligation to forgive us. In fact, you had every right to judge us. Yet you paid the debt we owe you through the precious blood of your son, Jesus. Remind us of this fact often so that we do not fall into self-righteous anger. Help us to forgive others as you have forgiven us. In your son's name, Jesus, we pray. Amen.

SEVEN
Adopted Son or Daughter

For he chose us in him before the creation of the world to be
holy and blameless in his sight. In love he predestined us to
be adopted as his sons through Jesus Christ, in accordance
with his pleasure and will to the praise of his glorious grace,
which he has freely given us in the One he loves... Having
believed, you were marked in him with a seal, the promised
Holy Spirit, who is a deposit guaranteeing our inheritance
until the redemption of those who are God's possession —
to the praise of his glory.
EPHESIANS 1:4-8, 13-14

Modern readers are quick to link this metaphor with present-day adoption practices. However, Roman adoption laws were different from ours. In the first century Roman world, families without a son could adopt an heir from another family. Also, an heir didn't wait for his father to die before receiving an inheritance.[18] An heir enjoyed joint ownership with his father over the family property.[19] Birth, not death, established heirship. Likewise, our new birth gains us entrance into God's family as his adopted sons and daughters. Paul describes this process in Romans 8:15-17:

You received God's Spirit when he adopted you as his own children. Now we call him, "Abba, Father." For his Spirit joins with our spirit to affirm that we are God's children. And since we are his children, we are his heirs.

Adoption gives us our status as co-heirs with Christ. And the Holy Spirit gives us assurance of our new status. In other words, God gives us the Spirit to show us he hasn't left us as orphans in this world (John 14:18).

If we cast our mind toward our future inheritance, the Bible projects a clear image of us co-reigning with Christ on a recreated earth filled with God's people. The image pixelates when we talk about the present benefits of our inheritance, however. What does it mean to live as co-heirs with Christ now? After all, God hasn't established his eternal kingdom yet. The New Testament tells us that we can experience the benefits of our inheritance through the Holy Spirit.

First, the Holy Spirit gives us unrestricted access to God. Paul explains that "because we are his children, God has sent the Spirit of his Son into our hearts, prompting us to call out, 'Abba, Father'" (Galatians 4:6).

Imagine one of your favorite musicians reached out to you and gave you her phone number. "Text or call any time," she insists. "It doesn't matter what it's about. I'm interested in hearing from you." You would feel honored to have this kind of access.

Yet Paul tells us we've gained unlimited access to the rightful ruler of the universe. And he eagerly awaits hearing from us. Other passages go even further, suggesting God desires to hear about the most mundane aspects of our lives. "Do not be anxious about anything, but in everything, by prayer and petition, with thanksgiving, present your requests to God" (Philippians 4:6).

Second, God's Spirit assures us of our future inheritance. God tells us this in Ephesians 1:13-14:

You also were included in Christ when you heard the message of truth, the gospel of your salvation. When you believed, you

were marked in him with a seal, the promised Holy Spirit, who
is a deposit guaranteeing our inheritance until the redemption
of those who are God's possession — to the praise of his glory.

In the ancient world, people used the word "guarantee" in commercial transactions to describe the first installment or deposit that went toward the purchase price of an item. It also secured legal claim of an item or validated a contract.[20] In the same way, God gives his Spirit as the first installment of our future inheritance.

The assurance that we will receive our heavenly inheritance reminds us to maintain a loose grip on our money and material possessions. It also frees us to take our eyes off of ourselves and to turn them onto others.

DELIBERATELY CHOSEN

Many adopted children today wrestle with identity issues. They struggle with feeling unwanted. They often wonder why their birth moms put them up for adoption.

Adoption in Roman society didn't carry the same stigma. In the ancient world, an adopted child enjoyed equal status with the biological children of that family. He had no reason to view himself as worthless or inferior. Indeed, New Testament scholar F.F. Bruce suggests the adoptee "might well enjoy the father's affection more."[21]

It was common for prominent families in the Roman world to cement ties through adoption. Families required a male heir to pass on the estate and name. If a family lacked one, it would seek to adopt a son from another. The family without an heir would choose the son with proven character and abilities. In a famous example, Julius Caesar adopted his 19-year-old nephew because he didn't have an heir. His nephew became the first Roman emperor, Augustus Caesar. This background brings to life Paul's statement in Ephesians 1:4-5. God purposely chose us. He marked us out before the creation of the world as his sons and daughters.

Some of us struggle with a sense of worthlessness. Feelings of inferiority cause us to go into reverse whenever God asks us to take a scary step of faith. Yet God placed incredible value upon us when he "predestined us to adoption before the creation of the world" (Ephesians 1:5). He sees the potential we have in Christ that we often fail to see in ourselves.

CANCELS DEBTS AND OBLIGATIONS

The adoptee received a new identity according to Roman adoption laws. His new status wiped away old obligations and debts. Paul picked a Greek word for redemption in the opening passage, which the Greco-Roman world used to describe settling an indentured servant's debt This snaps together with what Paul says about God's plan in Colossians 2:13-14: "He nevertheless made you alive with him, having forgiven all your transgressions. He has destroyed what was against us, a certificate of indebtedness."

God tore up our certificate of debt when he adopted us into his family. He bought back our freedom, giving us a new identity in Christ. He forgave all our sins so we don't have to face eternal judgment. Thus, our devotion springs from gratitude, not from guilt. He paid the ultimate price, sacrificing his one and only son to adopt us.

A few years ago, my friend was sharing an experience about adopting his son from Ethiopia. He and his wife spent tens of thousands of dollars on adoption and travel fees. They took several weeks off work, traveling back and forth from Ethiopia. And it took several years to finalize the process.

When my friend and his wife were finally ready to take their son home, he kept running away from them in the airport. He would approach complete strangers and beg them to take him home with them. My friend explained how he felt. "We were heartbroken. We spent a lot of money to adopt this child. We flew all the way to Ethiopia to get him. But all he wanted to do was get away from us."

Then it dawned on me: That's probably how God feels when we refuse to turn to him.

Our heavenly Father paid an incredible price to purchase a relationship with us. Therefore, we should take full advantage of the privilege he has conferred upon us through adoption as his sons and daughters.

Father, help us to see the privilege of our status as your adopted children. Help us to see the tremendous value you placed on us through the cross. Transform the way we view ourselves, so it fits with the reality of our new identity. Open the eyes of our hearts that we may see ourselves as co-heirs with Christ. Amen.

EIGHT
Child of God: Our Heavenly Father

How great is the love the Father has lavished on us, that we should be called children of God! And that is what we are! The reason the world does not know us is that it did not know him. Dear friends, now we are children of God, and what we will be has not yet been made known. But we know that when he appears, we shall be like him, for we shall see him as he is.

1 JOHN 3:1-2

A graduate student from India once came up to me after a Bible teaching with a puzzled look. "So, Christians relate to God the way a child relates to their father? Indian religions see God as removed from everyday life." He was baffled by this concept.

To some, it's difficult to wrap one's mind around the idea of God as a father at all. For others, it's harder to view him as *our* Father. Hearing the word "father" can bring to mind a variety of mental pictures. We tend to take our earthly fathers' flaws and superimpose them onto God. Yet God wants to overwrite our negative views as we get acquainted with him. This doesn't happen immediately. It takes time to build trust. We can start, however, by looking at some of the differences between our earthly fathers and our heavenly Father.

Many people I've talked to describe growing up with disengaged dads. They conjure up mental images of Dad sitting on the couch, zoned out in front of a screen after work. A long day at work left him too exhausted to relate. Others grew up with fathers who were mostly absent.

By comparison, God immerses himself in our lives. He indwells us with the Holy Spirit the moment we receive Christ. This event guarantees God's presence forever. His eye remains upon us from the moment we rise to the moment we lay our head down to sleep.

Scripture's view of God stands in sharp relief to many modern concepts of him. Most people in our culture believe God exists, but they think he wound up the universe and walked away. We can't say this about our heavenly Father. He wants to hear about what's whirring around in our heads. He even wants to hear about the most mundane aspects of our lives. He's never too busy to speak with us.

My children feel the liberty to interrupt me any time they want. I could be talking to a friend, and they will run up to me and blurt, "Daddy, look!" or, "Daddy, give me something to eat… now!" They will even grab my arm and swing on it like a monkey bar, just to get my attention. Everything feels urgent to them. It doesn't matter what I'm doing or who I'm talking to — my kids demand my undivided attention.

In the same way, God gives us the freedom to burst into his throne room with childlike faith. Paul explains that "because of Christ and our faith in him, we can now come boldly and confidently into God's presence" (Ephesians 3:12). Our heavenly Father invites audacious requests (Luke 11:5-8). Unlike our earthly fathers, God never feels too busy to talk with us or meet our needs. He never feels like we're interrupting.

God also desires intimate involvement in our lives. After all, he created every facet of our being. King David declares:

You created my inmost being; you knit me together in my

mother's womb… Your eyes saw my unformed body; all the days ordained for me were written in your book before one of them came to be. How precious to me are your thoughts, God! How vast is the sum of them! Were I to count them, they would outnumber the grains of sand. (Psalm 139:13, 16-18)

Can you imagine *anyone* thinking more about you than yourself? Yet, God's thoughts about you outnumber the grains of sand on a beach. He considers your needs, your feelings, your longings. His thoughts about you are innumerable.

SHOWS UNCONDITIONAL LOVE

God chose us before he laid the foundation of the earth. He planned to send Jesus long before we were born. God was aware of all the moral wrongdoings we would commit during our lifetimes and paid for them on a cross two thousand years ago. Thus, God doesn't withdraw his love from us when we fall into moral failure.

We never have to fear entering God's presence. Even when we sin, we can approach him with confidence. That's why the author of Hebrews urges, "Let us draw near to God with a sincere heart in full assurance of faith, having our hearts sprinkled to cleanse us from a guilty conscience and having our bodies washed with pure water" (10:22). He has washed away all our sins through Christ. Now we can boldly walk into his presence without shame, guilt or fear.

That's a far cry from how things work in our world. We live in a meritocracy — where advancement or rewards stem from merits such as performance, intelligence and education. Christian author Tim Keller makes this incisive cultural observation:

Success or failure is now seen as the individual's responsibility alone. Our culture tells us that we have the power to create ourselves, and that puts the emphasis on independence and self-reliance. But it also means that society adulates winners and despises losers, showing contempt for weakness.[22]

Many of us draw our sense of identity from success or failure. We see our value rising or falling based on our most recent performance. This leads us to feel as if we're bearing a tremendous weight of expectation — whether real or imagined — from those whose approval we desperately seek.

Our new identity, however, supplies us with a reliable anchor point. I've witnessed my kids do embarrassing things. I've seen them make lots of mistakes. I've watched them fail. Yet my love for them never changes. In the same way, God's approval of us doesn't fluctuate based on our performance, and he never looks on us with disappointment. He loves us because we are his children. Our heavenly Father's unchanging love offers the security we desire.

EAGER TO PROVIDE

Some of us didn't have a father around growing up. Some of us lived with our dad, but like a barnacle attached to a whale, he didn't contribute. He only took from our family. Our heavenly Father is different. He promises to meet our needs, and he has the resources to take care of us.

God even gave up his most prized possession to redeem us from the sentence of death. Paul asks, "He who did not spare his own Son, but gave him up for us all — how will he not also, along with him, graciously give us all things?" (Romans 8:32). Paul uses a style of argument that we don't use today. He's taking a lesser thing and comparing it to something greater: If this is true, then how much more must that be true? Following Paul's argument, if God didn't spare his beloved son to rescue us, how much more will he provide for our basic needs?

Some of us carry a crushing weight of anxiety. Our minds spin as we figure out how we're going to pay our bills. We stress about getting a career that will provide for a family. Thoughts of the future overwhelm us. Like a mortar and pestle, worry grinds us down as we attempt to meet our own needs.

It's a relief to know that God assumes that responsibility. We don't have to worry about how we're going to pay our rent or if we'll have enough money left in our pockets to eat. If we trust God and we're doing our part by working hard and limiting our spending, God will provide the rest if we come up short on our bills.

There have been times when my bank account was nearly empty and the due dates for several bills were approaching. I can't remember a time when God failed to provide. At times, he did it at the 11th hour, but he has always met my needs.

The same goes for a variety of areas that cause us worry. For singles, it might be the desire to get married. Our close friends and peers are getting engaged, and we're not even dating. Each year that goes by makes us more anxious about finding someone. At times, we feel tempted to step outside the lines of God's will and take matters into our own hands. Remember: God knows you and your desires. He will give you what you need if you wait for him to provide.

EMOTIONALLY ENGAGED

For some of us, our earthly father was involved. He played sports with us or took us fishing. He worked hard to provide. At the same time, he struggled to connect on an emotional level. He seemed uncomfortable talking about anything beyond the superficial. He would ask us about our day or talk about some interesting fact he discovered. But if we seemed depressed, he would utter a platitude or try to cheer us up by cracking a joke.

Our perfect heavenly Father doesn't suffer from fear of intimacy. If you want to glimpse God's eagerness to connect with you, examine Jesus' life. Jesus embodied God's ultimate revelation. God showed us more about himself through Jesus than through all the Old Testament prophets combined (John 14:8-9).

Jesus expresses a variety of emotions in the Gospels. Compassion arrested him when he encountered lost multitudes (Mark 6:34). He was unable to choke back sobs when he approached his friend Lazarus's tomb (John 11:35). His nurturing side came out when he took a small child in his arms (Mark 9:36-37).

Jesus experienced every human emotion that isn't a result of sin. He even felt the aching desire of temptation, though he never sinned (Hebrews 4:15). Therefore, God can relate to how you are feeling. He seeks to understand the thoughts swimming through your head. In fact, God's Spirit can take your scrambled thoughts and translate them into clear prayers (Romans 8:26).

CONCLUSION

God's children enjoy incredible security and significance. As we mature in our new identity, our confidence in his love grows, and our insecurities fade. Though we will never see complete victory over damage from our past until we see Jesus face to face, we can experience increased confidence in God's fatherly love and care.

Lord, you are a wonderful Father. You've never let me down. You've always been patient with me. You've always sought me out, even when I've tried to run from you. Thank you for your involvement in my life, and I look forward to the day when I get to spend the rest of eternity with you without any of the barriers or alienation that comes from my sin. Amen.

NINE
Child of God: Becoming Like Little Children

"I will be a father to you, and you shall be sons and daughters to Me," says the Lord Almighty.
2 CORINTHIANS 6:18

Jesus welcomed the presence of children. Most rabbis at this time treated them like a nuisance. Jesus admired certain qualities in them that he wanted his followers to adopt. At one point during Jesus' ministry, he motioned to a small child. Jesus said to his disciples:

"Truly I tell you, unless you change and become like little children, you will never enter the kingdom of heaven. Therefore, whoever takes the lowly position of this child is the greatest in the kingdom of heaven." (Matthew 18:2-4)

Jesus points to a paradox of spiritual growth: As we mature in Christ, we become more like children.

Now, Jesus doesn't want us engaging in infantile behavior. Toddlers display shameless self-centeredness, whereas God views others-centered love as the high-water mark of maturity (Galatians 5:6). Young children lack critical thinking, making them prone to deception and manipulation, but Scripture holds those who possess wisdom, knowledge and discernment in high regard (Ephesians 4:14). The Bible's greatest chapter on love says this, "When I was a child, I talked like a child, I thought like a child, I reasoned like a child. When I became a man, I put the ways of childhood behind me" (1 Corinthians 13:11).

Even so, Jesus often pointed to children as a model of humble faith. In this chapter, we will explore several childlike qualities that should appear as we grow into spiritual maturity.

CHILDREN READILY ADMIT INADEQUACY

Small children have a low tolerance for frustration. Spend time with a kid for one day. You will observe her ask for constant help. If her toy breaks, she will hand the pieces to you at the worst time and say, "Fix it!" If she can't open a package of food during lunch, she will thunder, "Open it!" Young children feel no shame in asking for assistance. Our heavenly Father desires for us to adopt this kind of humility.

Human beings are the only creatures on earth who are utterly helpless for their first year of life and heavily dependent on adult care for the next decade. In the same way, the essence of Christian living is dependence.

Adults devise sophisticated ways to fool themselves and others that they have everything under control, that they don't need anyone's help. Years of education, experience and maturity have taught adults to perform simple tasks such as opening a can of soup or operating a microwave. Nevertheless, they often walk around feeling bewildered and consumed by their problems. Most shoulder these burdens alone, refusing help or input.

God offers to bear our load. He never intended for us to direct our own path in life. He designed us to look to him for guidance. He fashioned us to rely on him for our needs. Our loving father eagerly awaits our requests for help.

WILLING TO RECEIVE GIFTS

Have you ever seen a child receive a gift and say, "Oh, I really can't accept this"? That's an adult response. Why are we reluctant to accept gifts? Probably because it makes us feel indebted to someone. Children, on the other hand, eagerly accept them and express elation when they unwrap presents.

In the same way, God wishes we would become like a little child and receive his grace without feeling like we must repay him with good deeds. Some of us struggle to relate to God because of this. We're unwilling to receive his grace. Rather than relate based on his graciousness, we try to convince him of how good we've been lately. We attempt to draw near to him, but our most recent wrongs flood our minds. We feel guilty about the way we have been living, as if good behavior earns us access to him.

God grants us an audience based on the gift his son purchased on the cross. And our uninterrupted access to him depends on his grace. Nothing else. No wonder God points to a small child and says, "I want you to become like her." He's asking us to set aside our pride and receive what we don't deserve.

STRONG BELIEF IN JUSTICE

In the late 2000s, millions of viewers eagerly awaited the weekly release of episodes from the critically acclaimed crime drama, *Breaking Bad*. Walter White, a high school teacher, discovers he has stage III cancer. He decides to pay for treatment by using his expertise in chemistry to cook methamphetamine.

Walter wrestles with the moral dilemma of his secret life under the alias Heisenberg. But he slowly embraces it and transforms into a ruthless criminal mastermind. You feel bad for him at first. By the end of the series, you're rooting for his downfall. Part of the show's widespread appeal was its moral ambiguity — a lack of certainty about right and wrong and whether characters are good or bad.

As modern Western people, we're comfortable with this. We spin someone's bad behavior by calling it "complicated" to justify our own moral compromise. We feel resistant to the idea of objective moral values that transcend time and culture. We recoil at the thought that we will be judged for our actions once we die.

Children see the world through a different lens.

In the 1920s, developmental psychologist Jean Piaget sat down on the floor and played a game of marbles to map moral development in young children. He found that as they develop a more sophisticated understanding of right and wrong, they go through a phase where they hold to "immanent justice" — the belief that certain kinds of behavior deserve certain kinds of punishment. At this stage, small children think that if they break rules, even accidentally, they will face negative consequences, even if nobody finds out.

Although God wants us to develop a category for gray areas and moral dilemmas, he also wants us to view the world through his eyes. When God looks at the world, he sees corruption, evil and rebellion. He calls his people to adopt his moral values and strong sense of justice. For example, Peter exhorts us:

> As obedient children, do not conform to the evil desires you had when you lived in ignorance. But just as he who called you is holy, so be holy in all you do; for it is written: "Be holy, because I am holy." (1 Peter 1:14-16)

It's natural to copy people we admire. As we spend more time with Jesus, we catch ourselves imitating his reaction to sin. God gradually makes us sensitive to evil as we mature. That's why Paul points to the virtue of justice as a mark of maturity (Titus 1:8).

A strong sense of God's justice also elevates our understanding of his graciousness. We're so familiar with grace that we come to expect it. It's often helpful to imagine what it would be like if God exercised his justice and didn't extend his grace. It helps us to grasp the magnitude of his mercy.

Several months ago, my oldest son broke my younger son's toy. Ren ran into my office with tears rolling down his face: "Julius broke my toy." Julius ran into the room a few seconds later repeating, "It was an accident. It was an accident."

Julius had been destroying things in our house. I had been warning him, "If you keep breaking things, we will make you pay for it." So we convened a family meeting.

I looked across the table and said, "Julius, you need to understand that there are consequences for your actions, even if it was an accident."

Then I turned to my younger son, "Ren, Julius has money to replace your broken toy. My question to you is this: Do you want him to pay for your broken toy, or are you willing to forgive him and live with your broken toy?"

I silently prayed, *God, I hope Ren gives Julius grace.* Ren paused for a second. I could see the gears turning.

"Julius needs to pay."

Well, that backfired, I said to myself. I looked across the table at my wife. Her eyes were as large as half-dollars. Julius stared down at the table, because it was going to cost him $30 to replace the toy.

I pressed my younger son again.

"Ren, you know God loves us a lot. He chooses not to make us pay for the bad things we've done even though we deserve to pay it ourselves. What do you want to do?"

"He needs to pay."

We're still working on the concept of God's grace. But Ren definitely gets justice.

What a relief that God doesn't exact justice but gives mercy. Although it's within his right to punish us for our sin, he paid for it.

LIVING IN THE PRESENT

Have you ever noticed that small children don't fret about the future or ruminate over the past? They live in the moment. This makes them carefree and unburdened.

Forecasting the future creates anxiety. Like chasing a desert mirage, we demand certainty because it gives us the illusion of control. No wonder Jesus soothes his anxious followers with these words, "Do not worry about tomorrow, for tomorrow will worry about itself. Each day has enough trouble of its own" (Matthew 6:34).

It's not just childlike to live in the moment — it's also a sign of faith. In the context of Jesus' statement, he was assuring his followers that God will provide for their basic needs. Even though this doesn't eliminate the need for careful planning or diligence (Proverbs 6:6-8), it does eliminate hand-wringing about our future. Remaining in the present frees us to enjoy life rather than worry about it.

Casting our minds on the past draws it away from the present. Reflection gathers lessons from the past; rumination anchors you to it. Paul resisted the temptation to fixate on his former life, "Forgetting what is behind and straining toward what is ahead, I press on toward the goal to win the prize for which God has called me heavenward in Christ Jesus" (Philippians 3:13-14). Eternity will provide endless opportunities to reflect. Living in the present prevents us from getting stuck and allows us to concentrate on serving others now.

UNINHIBITED

Rarely do you walk away from interactions with a small child wondering if he was making subtle jabs. Nor do you sit around speculating about a child's motives. A kid will say whatever is rattling around in his mind. There's no filter between a child's brain and his mouth.

I relish open communication with my children. As they get older, my sons may not talk to me about everything. They may be guarded at times.

Even though God wants us to develop discretion in the way we speak, he cherishes childlike honesty. Jesus loved Peter's honesty even though it sometimes got him in trouble (John 13:8-10).

As you grow into your identity in Christ, practice open communication with God. Talk with him about things that worry, frustrate, anger and excite you. If you find it easy to pray for others, set aside time to lay out how you are feeling. Be honest about things you want to accomplish and become, then listen to his responses.

UNLESS YOU BECOME...

The paradox of following Jesus is you become more childlike as you grow with him. God wants to wean you off autonomy and grow you in dependence. He desires to see you grow in humility, honesty, moral judgment and daily trust in him.

Father, I'm so grateful that you've chosen me to be your child. Develop in me the utter dependence and trust I see between a parent and a small child. I long to experience the kind of intimacy and tenderness that you shared with your own son, Jesus. Over time, I pray our relationship would be characterized by these qualities. Amen.

TEN
Child of God: Receiving Loving Discipline

And have you completely forgotten this word of encouragement that addresses you as a father addresses his son? It says, "My son, do not make light of the Lord's discipline, and do not lose heart when he rebukes you, because the Lord disciplines the one he loves, and he chastens everyone he accepts as his son."

Endure hardship as discipline; God is treating you as his children. For what children are not disciplined by their father? If you are not disciplined — and everyone undergoes discipline — then you are not legitimate, not true sons and daughters at all.

Moreover, we have all had human fathers who disciplined us and we respected them for it. How much more should we submit to the Father of spirits and live! They disciplined us for a little while as they thought best; but God disciplines us for our good, in order that we may share in his holiness. No discipline seems pleasant at the time, but painful. Later on, however, it produces a harvest of righteousness and peace for those who have been trained by it.

HEBREWS 12:5-11

The recipients of Hebrews were suffering intense persecution for their faith. So the author reminds them that what they're experiencing should be viewed as a form of God's discipline.

We live in a culture where parents rarely discipline their children. Boundaries are never established. Children are rarely denied what they want. When parents attempt to discipline, they often do so out of anger or frustration. Many of us were never disciplined growing up. Therefore, we have no category for it being helpful or loving.

But God's word insists that we're born with a corrupt nature. What seems right or good often proves to be damaging. Therefore, we need God's loving discipline to save us from ourselves.

GOD DISCIPLINES US FOR REDEMPTIVE PURPOSES

Some of us were disciplined growing up, but it wasn't redemptive. Discipline meant Dad or Mom finally had enough and snapped. They'd yell or hit us, but it wasn't meant to correct. It was a way for them to vent.

On the other hand, God isn't capricious. He doesn't fly off the handle and lash out, leaving us wondering what we did. When God disciplines believers, he does so out of love. Jesus paid for all of our moral guilt on the cross and once we receive his forgiveness, we don't have to worry about God punishing or being angry with us.

GOD CAN USE SUFFERING, ADVERSITY AND FAILURE TO DISCIPLINE US

I've heard people say in the midst of tragic suffering: "If God caused this, who am I to question it?" In other words, if something bad happened, God must've been behind it, since he's in control.

But God does not ordain the murder of innocent people. He does not compel sleazy con artists to scam confused elderly people. Individuals are ultimately responsible for their sin. God may permit evil in the world, though he never causes it. As James puts it:

When tempted, no one should say, "God is tempting me." For God cannot be tempted by evil, nor does he tempt anyone; but each person is tempted when they are dragged away by their own evil desire and enticed. Then, after desire has conceived, it gives birth to sin; and sin, when it is full-grown, gives birth to death. (James 1:13-15)

Humanity's misuse of free will brought sin into our world. God didn't cause this. He didn't want it to happen. Even so, Almighty God remains firmly in control of human history and promises to one day set everything right again. In his wisdom, he sovereignly laid out the course each of us is running (2 Timothy 4:7). That means he knew about and permitted the suffering and trials that would enter our lives. As the author of Hebrews explains, God uses hardship, persecution, failure and trials as a form of discipline.

GOD'S DISCIPLINE IS EVIDENCE OF HIS LOVE

Trials, persecution and vexing circumstances often do not feel like evidence of God's love. Usually, we feel confused about why God would allow suffering to enter our lives. The author of Hebrews affirms that "no discipline seems pleasant at the time, but painful," and assures us that, "God disciplines us for our good, in order that we may share in his holiness" (Hebrews 12:10).

When I discipline my children, I do it out of love. To prevent them from harming themselves. To teach them to respect authority and leadership. To avoid negative patterns of relating. But when they were little, however, they didn't understand. I would give them reasons why I put them in time out. Nevertheless, their minds struggled to grasp my explanation. Yet they knew I loved them.

In the same way, God's discipline is often confusing. We usually cannot see what God is trying to teach us while we're in the midst of a trial. Confusion often adds to our suffering.

The most important question you need to answer during times of suffering is not: *How could this happen?* It's not: *Why would God allow this suffering to enter my life?* The most important question is: *Do you trust that God loves you?*

We must remember who is in charge and what he wants — a gracious creator who desires for us to become like his son. God knows you better than you know yourself. He fashioned you in your mother's womb. He knows what's best. When God disciplines you, it's exactly what you need at just the right time.

Even though we may nod our heads when someone says that God disciplines us for our good, the process never feels good. God challenges us to fix our eyes farther downfield. He encourages us to persevere in faith so we can reap the "harvest of righteousness and peace for those who have been trained by it" (Hebrews 12:11).

Although God's discipline can cause excruciating pain, we can still feel joy in its throes. James mentions this strange paradox in his letter: "Consider it pure joy, my brothers and sisters, whenever you face trials of many kinds" (James 1:2). You might wonder how that's possible. How could it feel good to feel bad?

Christian author Randy Alcorn in his book, *Happiness*, explains how this works:

> Many have found happiness in times of hardship by anticipating the glory and goodness that await us, compared to which our present troubles are called "light and momentary" (2 Corinthians 4:17, NIV). A trapped miner, in pain from broken bones, can be overwhelmed with joy as he hears his rescuers making their way toward him — even though the actual rescue may not take place for hours or even days. Though knowing he'll still be suffering awhile, he rejoices that help is on its way.[23]

James finishes his thought about rejoicing amid suffering in a similar way, explaining that being tested through suffering produces endurance, and endurance brings greater spiritual maturity (James 1:3-4).

RESPONDING TO GOD'S DISCIPLINE

We often see things on a horizontal plane. During times of struggle, we tell ourselves, *People and circumstances are against me.* We didn't get a promotion because our boss doesn't like us. We're unhappy because the people around us aren't treating us right. Each time it seems like life is getting better, something else goes wrong.

As I write, many around the world have had their lives disrupted by a global pandemic which has claimed millions of lives. At times during the past year, I found myself spiraling into negativity, anger and frustration toward the restrictions we have had to face due to the virus. Everywhere I turn, it feels as if stay-at-home orders, curfews and gathering restrictions have blocked my best efforts to serve God.

But God spoke to me with clarity on several occasions in these dark moments. He unearthed something buried deep in my heart that only a global pandemic could expose. One evening as I was reading the book of Amos, God opened my eyes to his sovereignty. In Chapter 4, God describes how he used the natural disasters to lead the nation of Israel toward repentance.

> "Many times I struck your gardens and vineyards, destroying them with blight and mildew. Locusts devoured your fig and olive trees, yet you have not returned to me," declares the LORD.

> "I sent plagues among you as I did to Egypt. I filled your nostrils with the stench of your camps, yet you have not returned to me," declares the LORD. (Amos 4:8-10)

The Lord allowed drought, pestilence and disease to ravage the land so that Israel would see their need for him and return. God is sovereign. He is in control of all events in human history, including natural disasters.

If the Lord can use these things for his purposes, then he can use a global pandemic, too.

This opened my eyes to an important realization. I wasn't just angry and upset with my circumstances; I was angry and upset with God. If suffering and various trials fit with God's divine purposes, then I should not grumble when they enter my life.

Even though I felt as if this global pandemic ripped control from my hands, the fate of human history laid firmly within God's hands. The Lord was using this trial as a form of loving discipline. He not only showed me his sovereignty over nature; he also taught me to trust in his plan.

Placing your trust in God's ultimate control brings peace and contentment. It trains your eyes to see the many ways he has blessed you, which leads to the spontaneous expression of gratitude. It helps you focus on ways you can serve, rather than fixating on whatever negative circumstances you're facing.

Almighty Father, suffering tests our faith in your goodness. Often it feels as if our suffering is senseless. Yet you assure us in your word that you are sovereign and can use suffering as a form of loving discipline. Help us trust you during trials. Help us remain joyful. Help us persevere when we feel like quitting. Help us submit ourselves to your loving hand. We know that you are disciplining us for our good, so that we may share in your holiness. Amen.

ELEVEN
God's Friend

The LORD [would speak] to Moses face to face, as one
speaks to a friend.
EXODUS 33:11

Now if the ministry that brought death, which was engraved in
letters on stone, came with glory, so that the Israelites could not
look steadily at the face of Moses because of its glory, transitory
though it was, will not the ministry of the Spirit be even more
glorious?
2 CORINTHIANS 3:7-8

God desires a relationship with you. This is one of the most baffling aspects of Christianity. A recent Gallup poll claims that 87 percent of Americans believe in God.[24] However, I would guess that most hold faulty views of him. They view God as an exacting boss or a cosmic slot machine: Insert a good work, pull the lever and wait for blessings to rain.

By comparison, Scripture depicts God's relationship with us as the kind a loving father has with his children. Our heavenly Father provides everything we need. He gives us guidance for our lives. He even disciplines us in love when we need it.

Scripture goes even further. The Lord calls us his friend.

OUR GREAT PRIVILEGE IN CHRIST

Almighty God, the creator of our vast universe, condescends to call us his friend. It stretches the imagination to fathom how a transcendent God could view us this way.

Many of us have a favorite celebrity or sports figure. Imagine you got a phone call from an unknown number. You answer the phone, and the person claims to be the celebrity you admire.

"Someone entered your name in a drawing to meet me at my Los Angeles home. I've sent a car to your home to drive you to the airp…"

Click.

You hang up the phone. You say to yourself, *These scammers are getting more creative each day.* Two hours later, a limousine pulls into your driveway.

If it's a great honor to meet a celebrity or superstar athlete, how much more the creator of the universe? Scripture declares that God not only wants to meet us, he also wants to become our lifelong friend.

STABILITY

Friendships require effort and initiation from both sides. You may try your best to befriend someone, but a friendship will never form if the other person doesn't respond. You will never develop closeness if the person you are pursuing doesn't commit to spending time with you. Intimacy will disintegrate if you do not commit to work through conflict and hardship.

Unstable relationships make it difficult to draw near to people. You will be less likely to invest in one if you think it won't last. Nearly 50 percent of marriages in America end in divorce. Single-parent homes have quadrupled in the last 50 years. People move across the country for new job opportunities, uprooting their families and disrupting friendships. Instability creates insecurity. It causes you to be more guarded.

The Lord doesn't suffer from the shortcomings we see in our earthly friends. God offers us unparalleled security, promising never to leave us nor forsake us (Hebrews 13:5). He will always be at our side (Matthew 28:20). He's always faithful, even when we are not (2 Timothy 2:13). He actively pursues us even when we run from him, comparing himself to a shepherd who leaves 99 sheep in the pasture to find one that's lost (Luke 15:4). God continues to pursue and initiate even when we are closed off, patiently waiting for us to open the door and invite him in (Revelation 3:20). Christian author J. Oswald Sanders famously said, "You are as close to God as you choose to be."

INVESTMENT

Many followers of Jesus do not take full advantage of this great privilege. Preoccupation, ever-expanding responsibilities at work and growing demands at home leave little time for drawing near to God through prayer and reflection upon his word.

We need to view friendship with God as we do our other relationships. Quality bonds don't spontaneously form. They require investment and time spent.

Some wonder why they don't feel close to God. For most believers, the answer is failing to spend consistent time with him. Your relationships are only as good as the effort you put into them. If you don't make time, they won't be close.

INTIMACY

Carving out daily time with God represents a major step toward experiencing closeness. Yet we soon discover that consistent time doesn't guarantee intimacy. There are times when we feel as if God is distant or we cannot sense his presence. Why does this happen?

For one, God can feel intangible. We can't see him. Seldom does he speak with audible words. And during dry times he seems far off. But we cannot use our feelings as the only measure of closeness. Healthy relationships do not rest on feelings.

Take marriage, for instance. Marriages often begin with a period of infatuation, but marital bliss cannot carry couples through the many challenges life presents. Those who flourish invest when the feelings are not present.

Likewise, a profound sense of joy overwhelms most believers when they first place their faith in Christ. They feel his presence everywhere. This lasts for some time. However, when these overpowering emotions fade, dissonance sets in. These believers may feel as if their faith is falling apart; and yet, the opposite is happening. He's as close as he ever was. God is trying to teach them to live by faith and not by sight.

The prophet Isaiah encourages those who are "walking in darkness" to "trust in the Lord and rely on your God" (Isaiah 50:10). Jesus elevated the faith of those who seek him in the fog of doubt: "Blessed are those who have not seen and yet have believed" (John 20:29). Peter commends the faith of those who have not seen God, "Though you have not seen him, you love him; and even though you do not see him now, you believe in him and are filled with an inexpressible and glorious joy" (1 Peter 1:8).

Drawing near to God when feelings aren't present isn't a form of pretending. It's evidence of genuine faith. Strong emotions can shroud superficial faith, but times of dryness rip back the covers and expose it. If we persevere through these periods of confusion, God will awaken our spiritual need and deepen our faith.

Most failure to engage God is due to pride. Self-reliance impedes intimacy with God. Why isn't our instinct to talk with God when anxiety consumes us? It's because we don't see ourselves as dependent on him to meet our needs. We look to self instead.

Finally, lack of intimacy may stem from failing to recognize our privileged access to God. Some of us view him as a pathetic admirer who waits for a response to his bids for attention. We fail to see our utter unworthiness to enter the presence of the all-powerful creator of the universe.

The author of Hebrews states, "Brothers and sisters, since we have confidence to enter the Most Holy Place by the blood of Jesus let us draw near to God" (Hebrews 10:19, 22). Why would we need confidence to enter God's presence? Because it would be perilous for a rebel to stroll into the presence of a righteous king whose dominion extends over the Earth.

God's friendship offers profound peace and security. Drawing near to him fills the deep recesses of the soul. It quiets the inner voice of self-reproach that dictates what we do and how we treat others. It helps us to stop operating out of a deficit. It provides stability. It causes us to worry less about how others view us and to be ourselves. And it relieves the pressure we feel to live up to other's expectations or our own. Our friendship with God offers true stillness amid chaos.

Lord, what an immense privilege it is to be called your friend. I pray I would never take this for granted. Continue to reveal my unworthiness and expand my awareness of your greatness. Most of all, I pray that I would take full advantage of the unparalleled intimacy you offer in Christ. Amen.

TWELVE
God's Friend: Being a Good Friend

For since our friendship with God was restored by the death
of his Son while we were still his enemies, we will certainly be
saved through the life of his Son. So now we can rejoice in our
wonderful new relationship with God because our Lord Jesus
Christ has made us friends of God.
ROMANS 5:10-11 (NLT)

"This is my commandment: Love each other in the same way
I have loved you. There is no greater love than to lay down
one's life for one's friends. You are my friends if you do what
I command. I no longer call you servants, because a master
doesn't confide in his servants. Now you are my friends, since I
have told you everything the Father told me. You didn't choose
me. I chose you… This is my command: Love each other."
JOHN 15:12-17

Most ancient cultures had temples and priests. Ancient people went to
the temple because they saw the gap between them and the divine. They
utilized priests as mediators in an attempt to bridge that chasm. Priests
attempted to bring the divine near and appease the gods through ritual
sacrifices.

All such efforts were partial and fragmentary. No religion claimed to close the gap completely. Philosophers like Aristotle suggested that it was possible to venerate and temporarily appease the gods — but an intimate friendship with one was impossible. He argued that friendship requires that both parties be alike. Therefore, the possibility of friendship evaporates because the gods stand so far above humans.[25]

Then, Christianity appears on the scene with a preposterous claim: God put on human flesh and lived on the same plane of existence as us. This would've left ancient ears ringing with astonishment. How could anyone confidently approach God, much less be his friend?

Scripture teaches that God became like us in every respect, "in order that he might become a merciful and faithful high priest" (Hebrews 2:17). Jesus' humanity allowed him to play the role of both mediator and sacrifice — a priest putting himself forward as a perfect offering. This not only enabled us to enter God's presence, it also made a friendship with him possible.

As we said earlier, God does not suffer from the shortcomings of our friends. He's a faithful friend, who does more than his share in the relationship. Now, we will shift our attention to what we can do to strengthen our friendship with him.

LISTENING

Listening plays a crucial role here, just as it does in human friendships. Careful consideration leads to mutual understanding. Some people don't realize that closeness doesn't always require talking. Christian author John White applies this to prayer when he writes, "Prayer must never be a monolog."[26] Think about how you feel after spending several hours with a friend who never lets you get a word in. That's probably how God feels when we talk at him.

James directs us toward God when we feel confused: "If you need wisdom, ask our generous God, and he will give it to you" (James 1:5). The Lord freely gives insight to anyone who asks. In other words, if we ask, we must wait for his response.

Daily distractions prevent us from hearing the subtle leading of the Spirit. Phone notifications arrest our attention like a Pavlovian bell. Glowing devices mesmerize our screen-soaked retinas. It takes conscious effort to practice listening prayer. We may not immediately hear his voice when we ask for wisdom. Hearing from God takes patience and persistence.

We shouldn't expect that hearing from God will take the form of a mystical experience — where God appears in a vision or dream. Scripture teaches that God's word represents his active presence in the world (Isaiah 55:10-11). Christian author and thinker Tim Keller states, "To say that God's word goes out to do something is the same as to say God has gone out to do something."[27]

God so identifies himself with his words that when we interact with them, we interact with him. In his book, *Words of Life*, theologian Timothy Ward writes, "Communication *from* God is therefore communion with God, when met *with* a response of trust from us" (emphasis mine).[28]

Thus, hearing from God takes place in a broader context of an ongoing dialogue. It takes into consideration previous interactions and what he has already communicated through his written word. Scripture is the vocabulary through which God speaks to us.

Here's how this looks from my experience. I may enter a time with God feeling distraught or confused, so I ask God for insight. Sometimes I leave that time of prayer with a vague impression of his answer. It's not clear. As I read Scripture, I may notice something that addresses my confusion. Or a passage may come to mind as I'm thinking about what's bothering me. God may even provide some clarity as I talk about it with a trusted Christian friend. Then, I return to God in prayer. It may take days or weeks before gaining clarity. Like slight adjustments on a camera focus ring, the picture comes into focus each time I return in prayer.

Though God may clarify our confusion at times, it's not the ultimate goal (Job 42:3). Knowing God better is the goal. The process of speaking and listening to him in the midst of confusion is one of many ways God draws us closer. That's why times of struggle and confusion often mark periods of profound spiritual closeness.

CONFIDING

Modern Americans have grown more isolated each year. According to a 1990 study, only a third of Americans had three or fewer close friends, and three percent had no close friends.[29] Things are much worse today. A similar survey in 2021 found that half of Americans had three or fewer close friends, and 12 percent had no one they could confide in.[30] That's heartbreaking: Almost 40 million people in America don't have anyone they can turn to during difficult times.

As humans, we long for meaningful connection. We're looking for someone we can trust who will listen to our innermost thoughts. Many of our interactions tend to be superficial. We can exchange information about ourselves without much self-disclosure.

Some of our conversations, however, go deeper. We sense in those moments that we are not just revealing information. The conversation becomes a personal encounter.[31] Close friends feel the freedom to share personal details, such as their anxieties and fears, without worry of judgment or rejection.

Likewise, God invites us to talk to him about what's bothering us. He assures us that, no matter what we share, it will not change his view of us (Romans 8:38-39). We have a trusted friend in Jesus. He encourages us to pour out our hearts to him.

God wants us to tell him how we feel about him. King David opens a window in Scripture for us to see the honest and raw interactions he had with God: "I pour out my complaints before him and tell him all my troubles" (Psalm 142:2). Christian author and speaker Rick Warren comments on the strident tone used when biblical characters speak to God.

> Can God handle that kind of frank, intense honesty from you? Absolutely! Genuine friendship is built on disclosure. What may appear as *audacity* God views as *authenticity*. God listens to the passionate words of his friends; he is bored with predictable, pious clichés. To be God's friend, you must be honest to God, sharing your true feeling, not what you think you ought to feel or say.[32]

Some of you lack intimacy with God because you are not being honest with him. It's likely you may be disappointed, angry or even bitter because of unanswered prayers, past hurts or present circumstances. If so, be honest, but respectful. Unless you address your controversy with God, you will remain distant from him.

On the other side, God confides in us as he would a friend. Jesus made the astounding statement: "I have called you friends, for everything that I learned from my Father I have made known to you" (John 15:15). God's self-disclosure in Scripture and the Holy Spirit's role in illuminating truth prove that God has brought us into his inner circle. The delight of discovering a new insight from the Bible is him confiding in us as a friend. Grasping the significance of a spiritual truth that we have merely stored in our minds is God revealing "spiritual realities with Spirit-taught words" (1 Corinthians 2:13). Only God's friends have access to this kind of understanding.

As we move forward, we shouldn't discount the ways God confides in us day to day as we wait for an audible voice, dream or vision. God lavishes wisdom upon us as he makes known the mystery of his will through Scripture (Ephesians 1:8-9). We should rejoice each time we are able to grasp something new.

Most of us don't sit around wondering if we're obeying our friends. Yet our friendship with God is far from normal. Almighty God lowered himself to befriend us. Further, we must define obedience within the context of Jesus' words.

> "This is my commandment: Love each other in the same way I have loved you. There is no greater love than to lay down one's life for one's friends. You are my friends if you do what I command." (John 15:12-14)

To obey Jesus is to love others. As with all God's commands, he calls us to do what's best for others while ultimately doing what's best for us.

Unlike our earthly friendships, God does not expect us to play an equal part in the friendship. If you poured everything into a relationship but never got anything back, you would wonder if it was worth being that person's friend. Not so with God. He never expects us to give back to him. He's the eternal giver. Instead, he takes delight in us loving others.

As with any good friendship, spending time with God will influence our thinking and our values. The greatest sign of closeness with God is our growing love for others.

Father, thanks that you sent your son, Jesus, to pay the immense cost of granting me access to you in prayer. What a wonderful privilege it is to talk to you without fear or guilt. I pray, Lord, that I can do my part to strengthen and grow our friendship. Amen.

THIRTEEN
Bearer of a New Name

God places a high value on community. He promises we will find happiness as we play our role within it. But he also values our uniqueness and individuality.

Today, we give children names to provide a sense of identity. Sometimes, we name a child to honor or commemorate a loved one. Other times, we name our child something uncommon because it's unique.

In the ancient world, names took on greater significance. A name told a story. Abraham and Sarah named their son Isaac, which means "laughter" in Hebrew. They did this because Sarah laughed when God promised they would have a son in their old age.

Later, Isaac and his wife, Rebekah, named their twin sons after qualities that would define them.

> When the time came for her to give birth, there were twin boys in her womb. The first to come out was red, and his whole body was like a hairy garment; so they named him Esau. After this, his brother came out, with his hand grasping Esau's heel; so he was named Jacob. (Genesis 25:24-26)

Esau's name sounds like the Hebrew word for "hairy." Jacob's name literally means "heel," which can also mean "to deceive."

At the end of Isaac's life, Jacob conned his father into blessing him with Esau's birthright. When Esau discovered what happened, he exclaimed, "Isn't he rightly named Jacob? This is the second time he has taken advantage of me: He took my birthright, and now he's taken my blessing!" (Genesis 27:36).

Today, Western people look to unique traits or skills to define who they are. They loathe the idea of being ordinary. "Blending in" and "just playing your part" are tantamount to losing your identity.

Although Scripture rejects the individualism that dominates society, it celebrates each individual in God's family (1 Corinthians 12:12-26). To signify our uniqueness, Jesus even promises to give us a new name. He writes this to the church at Pergamum, "To the one who is victorious, I will give… that person a white stone with a new name written on it, known only to the one who receives it" (Revelation 2:17).

In some cases, God gave people a new name to symbolize their new identity. Near the close of his life, Jacob found himself wrestling with God at the banks of a river. The Lord overpowered him after hours of struggle, but Jacob clung to him and refused to let go until God blessed him. The Lord agreed, "Your name will no longer be Jacob, but

Israel, because you have struggled with God and with humans and have overcome" (Genesis 32:28).

Jacob's new name indicated an internal shift. Throughout his life, he connived and manipulated to get his way. He lived up to his name, the Deceiver. Perhaps Jacob credited his success and great wealth to his cunning and hard work, though Scripture tells us it was actually God blessing him (Genesis 27, 30).

Jacob limped away from that encounter a changed man. God had finally broken him of his self-reliance. Israel means something like "God fights" or "triumphant with God." The name signified that he would no longer rely on human striving to succeed. Instead, he would rely on the Lord to fight for him.

Fast forward to the New Testament. Jesus renames Simon, "Peter," after seeing a remarkable display of Simon's faith. Peter was the first of Jesus' disciples to identify him as God's Chosen One. The Greek word for Peter, *petros*, means "rock." Jesus explains that he would make Peter the stable foundation upon which he would build his church (Matthew 16:18).

If you trace Peter's life throughout the gospels, you immediately notice that he was not a stable person. His emotions drove him. One moment he's summiting the mountaintop of spiritual insight by proclaiming that Jesus is the son of God (Mark 8:27-29). The next he's rebuking Jesus after he reveals that he must suffer many things and be killed (Mark 8:31). One moment he defends Jesus with a sword against the soldiers who came to arrest him (John 18:10). The next he denies even knowing Jesus when a young woman questions him (Mark 14:68). You see, Jesus peered past Peter's emotional volatility and saw the stability that would make him the most prominent leader of the early church.

By contrast, some of us form our sense of identity around our failures. We allow our problems, struggles and tendencies to define us. Yet God doesn't see what we see looking back at us in the mirror. God can look past our sinful tendencies and see our new identity in Christ. The Lord works from eternity, toward eternity, to accomplish his desired goal. That's how he maintains a vision for our transformation. Therefore, you are contradicting God when you despair over your sin. Telling yourself you will never change is tantamount to telling God, "I don't share your vision for my transformation."

Let's go back to Peter. His life illustrates God's power to change our character. Peter shows courage and fortitude in the book of Acts that he lacked during Jesus' ministry. Acts 4 tells us that the Jewish leaders in Jerusalem seized Peter and John for proclaiming that Jesus rose from the dead. Rather than cowering, Peter declared the gospel to the Jewish rulers.

> When they saw the courage of Peter and John and realized that they were unschooled, ordinary men, they were astonished and they took note that these men had been with Jesus. (Acts 4:13)

The Jewish leaders warned Peter not to speak or teach about Jesus under threat of judgment. Peter fired back: "Which is right in God's eyes: to listen to you, or to him? You be the judges! As for us, we cannot help speaking about what we have seen and heard" (Acts 4:19-20).

What a wonderful picture of transformation. Jesus was able to fulfill his vision. He changed this unstable man into a solid foundation for the church.

Finally, we come under God's authority when he gives us a new name. If you renamed someone in the ancient world, it meant you were placing your authority over that person. The Lord commanded the first man to exercise dominion over the earth through taxonomy, categorizing and naming the animal life he saw. Likewise, almighty God gives us a new name to symbolize that he's placed his authority over us. We've come under his loving rule.

Many Christians refuse to submit their lives to God. Their self-will stands in the way of their spiritual growth. Over time, they become deluded in their thinking. Their values mimic the world's, rather than God's.

This stiff-necked response to God stands at odds with our new identity in Christ. Our new name signifies our submission to him. God wants us to yield to him as Jacob, Peter and many other biblical figures did. He assures us that if we submit to him, we no longer need to strive and meet our own needs. Instead, God will meet our basic needs and our deepest longings.

Lord, you created my inmost being and fashioned me in my mother's womb. You have searched me and know me. More than this, you make me even more unique in Christ. You gave me a name that's only known to me. This highlights the kind of care and individual love you have for me. Teach me to trust you. Bring circumstances into my life to break me of my self-sufficiency. Help me see that a life yielded to you is a life filled with happiness. Amen.

FOURTEEN
Bearer of God's Family Name

Consequently, you are no longer foreigners and strangers, but fellow citizens with God's people and also members of his household.
EPHESIANS 2:19

"Bring my sons from afar and my daughters from the ends of the earth — everyone who is called by my name, whom I created for my glory, whom I formed and made."
ISAIAH 43:6-7

God decided in advance to adopt us into his own family by bringing us to himself through Jesus Christ.
EPHESIANS 1:5 (NLT)

In more traditional cultures, one's family name carries weight. People assume things about you when they hear it. I visited the Philippines when I was a teenager. My family stayed at the home where my mother grew up. Her family lived in this neighborhood for three generations. When I walked around, I noticed something odd. The people I met seemed more interested in my mother's maiden name than my given name.

"Ahh, so you're a Bacay," they would say.

It seemed as if knowing my family told them all they needed to know about me. Some would say, "They are a good family," and recount how my grandfather helped their brother many years ago. Growing up in the United States, no one ever asked me for my family name unless I was filling out a form.

Likewise, God puts his family name upon us when we place our faith in Christ. Bearing his name makes us part of his family and becomes part of our new identity.

Isaiah predicted God would gather his people from among the nations and form them into a family. "Bring my sons from afar and my daughters from the ends of the earth," God told the prophet Isaiah, "everyone who is called by my name, whom I created for my glory, whom I formed and made" (Isaiah 43:6-7).

The author of Hebrews assures us that God made us holy and that "those who are made holy are of the same family" (Hebrews 2:11). John the Apostle gives us a glimpse into this future reality in the book of Revelation when God establishes the New Heavens and New Earth. "They will see his face," he writes, "and his name will be on their foreheads" (Revelation 22:4).

A STABLE IDENTITY

Modern people recoil at the idea of something external giving us our sense of identity. We define our identity. We decide the meaning and purpose of our life, not our family or our community. That's why we see traditional culture as stifling. It suppresses an individual's hopes, dreams and desires.

Yet we're not as immune to the external world molding our sense of identity as we would like to think. Even though we would say we define our own identity, culture largely dictates our beliefs and values that determine our core identity.

Consider the importance of tolerance in our society. Most people like to see themselves as open-minded and accepting of all people. In fact, the only thing our culture is intolerant of is intolerance. And yet, how did nearly everyone in our culture decide on their own that tolerance is the supreme virtue? Why was intolerance toward minority groups not only accepted but even reinforced in certain parts of America just 60 years ago? Sociologist Robert Bellah calls this idea of creating our own sense of identity in isolation "a powerful cultural fiction." "We are most coerced," he observes, "by the dominant beliefs of our own culture."[33]

In truth, we need something or someone outside of ourselves to validate our sense of identity. If you aspire to become a world-renowned architect, you're relying on recognition from your colleagues. To become an influencer, you need followers and sponsors. You see, nothing has changed. We can't bestow significance upon ourselves. We've simply shifted the need for validation from family or community to our peers. And our sense of self-worth will fluctuate based on their approval.

Fortunately, God gives us an identity based on something stable and unchanging: his eternal name (Psalm 135:13). When we take God's name, we become a child in his family. That means God bestows significance upon us, not on the basis of our performance, but because he placed his seal of approval onto us through his son (John 6:27).

FAMILY, FREEDOM AND INDIVIDUALISM

In most cultures, your individual interests are not distinct from the good of your family. Just the opposite. Individual achievement brings honor to your family. Growing up, I would go to large Filipino gatherings and hear proud parents take turns talking about their kids' achievements. My parents just smiled and nodded. In most parts of the world, you form your sense of identity around being a good son, daughter, father or mother.

Modern Western people see traditional culture as something that impedes freedom, which they deem the highest good. Christian author Tim Keller argues that modern man sees becoming free as "the only heroic story we have left, and that giving individuals freedom is the main role of any institution and of society itself."[34] Modern people have redefined freedom as the choice to do whatever you want. But freedom defined as an absence of constraints isn't true freedom.

In reality, we have numerous freedoms that often collide. For example, I enjoy long bike rides. They allow me to decompress after a busy day and get me outside. I also cherish playing with my young children. My window of opportunity to do this closes each year as they get older. Both riding my bike and spending time with my kids bring me enjoyment. My busy schedule, however, often forces me to decide between the two. The choice isn't difficult, I choose to spend time with my kids.

Freedom isn't a single commodity that you either have or don't have. We have many different freedoms, that at times, conflict. As Keller aptly stated: "Real freedom comes from a strategic loss of freedoms in order to gain others."[35]

You see, our world's definition of freedom is largely negative, it's the free-dom *from* something. However, Scripture defines freedom positively, it's freedom *for* something. Paul makes it clear that God purchased our freedom in Christ so that we might love others. "You, my brothers and sisters, were called to be free. But do not use your freedom to indulge the flesh; rather, serve one another humbly in love" (Galatians 5:13).

A healthy, functioning family works if everyone agrees to, at times, set aside their own rights for the good of others. What if everyone in God's family showed a willingness to sacrifice their desires for the sake of others? What if we did not merely look to our own interests, but also for the interests of others? What if we made it our ambition to do what was best for others in God's family? It would make Jesus' request to the Father a reality.

"I pray also for those who will believe in me through their message, that all of them may be one, Father, just as you are in me and I am in you. May they also be in us so that the world may believe that you have sent me. I have given them the glory that you gave me, that they may be one as we are one — I in them and you in me — so that they may be brought to complete unity. Then the world will know that you sent me and have loved them even as you have loved me." (John 17:21-23)

GLORIFYING GOD'S NAME

As those who bear God's name, we should behave in such a way that brings honor and avoids casting shame on it. This means being mindful of how our words and actions reflect on God's name. The watching world formulates its view of God largely by the behavior of his followers.

Most Americans associate the word "Christian" with hypocrisy. People don't even bat an eye when they hear about the latest sex scandal involving a prominent Christian pastor. I've sat and listened to countless non-believing people recount how a negative encounter with a Christian left a bad impression.

The same problem plagued the church in the first century. Paul the Apostle scolded the Roman believers for how their hypocrisy left a mark on God's name. "You who brag about the law, do you dishonor God by breaking the law?" he asks in Romans 2:23. "As it is written: 'God's name is blasphemed among the Gentiles because of you.'" Followers of Jesus should be as warm and approachable as the Lord was during his ministry.

We also honor God's name when we love those who show hostility toward Christianity. Peter advises us to live such good lives among our non-Christian neighbors that even when they accuse us of doing wrong, they may see our good deeds and attribute them to God (1 Peter 2:12). God uses our actions to thaw people's hearts and create openings for the gospel.

Finally, we bring glory to God's name as people witness the love we share as God's family. God's love is reflected in an engaged family that invites someone who grew up in a broken home over for a meal. Or when a non-Christian person walks into a room filled with believers and is greeted with warmth and acceptance.

Jesus made it clear he didn't want his followers to form a cloister. He wanted our love to be visible to those who do not know him. He wanted our love for one another to act as a beacon, directing people to the gospel. We bring glory and honor to God's name as we play a small part in leading people to Jesus through our words and actions:

> Through Christ, God has given us the privilege and authority as apostles to tell Gentiles everywhere what God has done for them, so that they will believe and obey him, bringing glory to his name. (Romans 1:5)

Lord, what a privilege to bear your name. I'm grateful that you let me into your family. I pray that you would refine the American church. I pray that one day its good deeds would bring honor to your name, rather than shame and reproach. I pray that I can play my small part in bringing glory to your family name. Help me to be mindful of how I represent your name to the watching world. Amen.

FIFTEEN
One in Christ

There is neither Jew nor Gentile, neither slave nor free, nor is there male and female, for you are all one in Christ Jesus.
GALATIANS 3:28

For Christ himself has brought peace to us. He united Jews and Gentiles into one people when, in his own body on the cross, he broke down the wall of hostility that separated us. He did this by ending the system of law with its commandments and regulations. He made peace between Jews and Gentiles by creating in himself one new people from the two groups. Together as one body, Christ reconciled both groups to God by means of his death on the cross, and our hostility toward each other was put to death... Now all of us can come to the Father through the same Holy Spirit because of what Christ has done for us.
EPHESIANS 2:14-18 (NLT)

Theists and atheists alike would say that all men and women are equal. But this raises the question: *In what sense are we equal?*

What makes a white, male millionaire from Manhattan equal to a Mexican woman from East Los Angeles? What makes a child with Down syndrome equal to a professor of economics at a top college?

The concept of equality hinges upon human value. All men and women are equal — regardless of race, class or cognitive ability — because we view human life as precious.

Yet how do you derive human value from a naturalistic worldview? If we're just bags of biological material sloshing around, in what sense are we significant? How does equality fit within the overall landscape of naturalism? Some might say, "A certain level of cooperation was necessary to survival and reproduction." Though natural selection describes some of what happens in the world, it cannot tell us how we ought to behave. It certainly doesn't give humans intrinsic value.

In contrast to naturalism, the biblical view teaches that God created all men and women in his image (Genesis 1:27). This gives humans inherent value no matter their race, gender or socio-economic standing. God expects us to value all people and treat them with dignity because humans bear his image.

Believers share even greater commonality than being his image-bearers. God has made us one in Christ and transforms our minds to embrace his values and views. As a result, he insists we repent of the racism and mistreatment of the poor and women common throughout the world.

UNITY IN DIVERSITY IN THE NEW TESTAMENT CHURCH

The Holy Spirit gave birth to the church in Acts 2 when Peter spoke to the multitudes gathered on the day of Pentecost, an important festival in the Jewish calendar. In the first century, Jewish people would travel to the Temple in Jerusalem to offer a gift of thanksgiving to God by bringing the first part of their harvest. Luke notes that "there were staying in Jerusalem God-fearing Jews from every nation under heaven" when suddenly Peter began to proclaim the good news of Jesus, the "crowd came together in bewilderment, because each one heard their own language being spoken" (Acts 2:6). People from 16 nations stood captivated by the message of Christ. Three thousand people responded to Jesus that day. The early church began as a racially diverse, spiritual community. God wants that to continue today.

Now, racial diversity isn't always possible in certain parts of the world. How can you achieve it in Seoul or Shanghai? Diversity, though, isn't limited to race. In ethnically homogeneous parts of the world, God forms diverse churches among the rich and poor.

For instance, wealthy and impoverished believers shared fellowship with one another in the early church. The ancient world saw a stunning contrast between the rich and the poor. Yet God moved the hearts of wealthy believers to show compassion and radical generosity for impoverished believers. Luke points to the remarkable unity and sacrificial love in the early church. "All the believers were together and had everything in common," he writes, and the wealthy believers "sold property and possessions to give to anyone who had need" (Acts 2:44-45).

God's Spirit unified rich and poor in the early church, and oneness in Christ provided the basis for combatting partiality. James calls out his audience for showing favoritism toward the rich while snubbing the poor. He asks them this stinging rhetorical question: "Has not God chosen those who are poor in the eyes of the world to be rich in faith and to inherit the kingdom he promised those who love him?" (James 2:5). Showing preference to the rich contradicts our oneness in Christ, since the cross flattens the social stratification that divides people.

DIVERSITY IN THE NEW HEAVENS AND NEW EARTH

The diversity in the church is a small sample of the diversity we will enjoy in heaven. The Apostle John pulls back the curtain and gives us a glimpse of God's throne room in Revelation 5:9-10.

> They sang a new song, saying: "You are worthy to take the scroll and to open its seals, because you were slain, and with your blood

you purchased for God persons from every tribe and language and people and nation. You have made them to be a kingdom and priests to serve our God, and they will reign on the earth."

Heaven will contain people groups from every nation. You will hear various languages as you walk the streets of the New Jerusalem. Unlike many major cities throughout the world, the New Jerusalem will not contain pockets of impoverished areas that divide residents along socio-economic lines. Instead, those who suffered poverty in this life will relate to those who were rich without shame or envy. Those who were rich in this life will speak to those who were impoverished without an air of superiority or even a whiff of haughtiness. The cross of Jesus will be the great equalizer for everyone in the New Heavens and on the New Earth.

EVIDENCE THAT JESUS IS GOD'S SON

Diversity is one of the main goals in modern society. Scripture would agree that diversity is important — yet it isn't the primary goal of the church. Glorifying God is. The church's diversity should stand out as a unique feature of the unity believers share in Jesus.

This idea of unity in diversity finds its greatest expression within the Godhead. The Trinity is comprised of three distinct persons who share a single identity and nature. God the Father, God the Son and God the Holy Spirit enjoyed perfect unity before the creation of the world.

Several hours before Jesus' arrest and crucifixion, he prayed to the Father that we might experience the unity they have shared from all eternity.

> "I pray also for those who will believe in me through their message… that they may be one as we are one — I in them and you in me — so that they may be brought to complete unity. Then the world will know that you sent me and have loved them even as you have loved me." (John 17:21-23)

The unity in diversity present in the church mirrors the unity in diversity within the Trinity.

Although diversity isn't the overarching goal of the church, it gives a foretaste of the diverse community we will experience in heaven. It also broadens our opportunities to reach people for Christ.

LOOKING PAST OUR DIFFERENCES

Researchers who study religious communities found a high turnover rate among minorities in majority white churches.[36] Minorities and people from under-resourced backgrounds often struggle with feeling like outsiders in most American churches.

Dwell Community Church has grown in diversity over the past two decades. When I first started attending, I was one of a dozen minority members in a church with thousands in attendance each week. I spent most of my life in Chicago, living in a diverse neighborhood on the north side of the city. And as mentioned earlier, I got into a lot of trouble when I was younger.

So I walked into my first large gathering at Dwell with my guard up. Something happened as I listened to the Bible teaching. God's word captivated me. I had never heard Scripture presented with such depth and relevance. Despite the obvious differences between me and the people I met that evening, God's word drew me in. I was still skeptical that anyone there would be able to relate to my situation.

My perception changed when a guy from our college ministry invited me to get lunch on the Ohio State University campus. He was a big white guy who played football in high school. He came from an affluent family and attended wealthy suburban schools. As I listened to the story of how he came to Christ, I found myself resonating with the feelings of despair and emptiness he described right before he turned to Jesus.

God showed me that although no one can fully understand what you've been through, they can relate to how you felt in those moments. The combination of sitting under Bible teaching and the freedom to be vulnerable without fear of judgment kept me coming back. Over time, I realized I had more in common with believers from different backgrounds than I shared with people I had known for many years.

Our unity goes even further. God unites us in purpose as we carry out his mission of sharing the message of Christ and developing disciples (Matthew 28:18-20). According to Scripture, we're engaged in a spiritual struggle against God's enemy, Satan, who holds the world captive through deception and fear (Hebrews 2:14-15). Nothing binds individuals together more than fighting a common enemy.

Lord, I praise you for the unity of the Spirit. It amazes me that I can meet a believer from New York or Port-au-Prince and experience the commonality that comes from knowing Christ. I'm excited to see you grow the diversity in the American church, so that it will dimly reflect the New Jerusalem, where people from every nation and people group will praise you in their own languages. Amen.

SIXTEEN
Body of Christ

The body is a unit, though it is made up of many parts; and though all its parts are many, they form one body. So it is with Christ. For we were all baptized by one Spirit into one body — whether Jews or Greeks, slave or free — and we were all given the one Spirit to drink.
1 CORINTHIANS 12:12-13

For just as each of us has one body with many members, and these members do not all have the same function, so in Christ we, though many, form one body, and each member belongs to all the others. We have different gifts, according to the grace given to each of us.
ROMANS 12:4-6

Christ himself gave the apostles, the prophets, the evangelists, the pastors and teachers, to equip his people for works of service, so that the body of Christ may be built up until we all reach unity in the faith and in the knowledge of the Son of God and become mature, attaining to the whole measure of the fullness of Christ…Instead, speaking the truth in love, we will grow to become in every respect the mature body of him who is the head, that is, Christ. From him the whole body, joined and held together by every supporting ligament, grows and builds itself up in love, as each part does its work.
EPHESIANS 4:11-13, 15-16

The church is not an institution; it's an organism. Believers are not united by formal membership or attendance at a local church. We are united by our connection to Christ. God joins us with Christ the moment we place our faith in him, and by extension he unites us with other believers. Students of Scripture call this the mystical union. The presence of God's Spirit gives us a common bond with Christians throughout the world. That means we share a deep spiritual connection with others that extends beyond our local spiritual community.

We are not responsible to create unity with other followers of Jesus. We don't need to find a common cause around which we should rally. Instead, God calls on us to "make every effort to keep yourselves united in the Spirit, binding yourselves together with peace" (Ephesians 4:3, NLT). What is God commanding us to do in this verse? He isn't telling us to make every effort to unify ourselves with other believers. He tells us to *keep* ourselves united in the Spirit. In other words, we do not need to drum up feelings of unity for other believers. It's ours in Christ. As followers of Jesus, we have a unique basis for unity. Our job is to preserve it.

DIVERSE GIFTING

God doesn't stamp out Christians on an assembly line. He endows each member with a different set of spiritual gifts. He arranges the body of Christ so that each member contributes something unique to its overall function.

This argues against a man-centered church. Many ailing churches see a constant turnover of leadership. Each time this happens, the church assembles a search committee that looks for a dynamic preacher or someone with remarkable leadership gifting to carry the church toward a successful future. No doubt, God uses gifted leaders and teachers to expand his kingdom.

However, basing the operation and growth of the entire church on a single gifted person would be like having a massively enlarged heart. It would not be a sign of health; it would be a symptom of a grave problem.

The key to spiritual growth isn't to find the best preacher or leader. The body of Christ "grows and builds itself up in love, as each part does its work" (Ephesians 4:16). Just like a human body, the church grows as each member contributes.

No programs or quick-fix solutions will accomplish this. It will take a concerted effort from the church's leadership to equip and build up its members for "works of service." It will require giving members significant roles to play in the church. It means each of us must show up at spiritual gatherings with an attitude to serve.

I once heard someone say that the modern American church resembles an NBA game: 10 people on the floor in desperate need of rest and 20,000 people in the stands in desperate need of exercise.

God has uniquely gifted you in some way. The only way to discover your gifting is to serve in various ways. You may not realize you have a gift of mercy till you serve the poor. You may not realize you are gifted at sharing your faith until you try. Discovering and developing your spiritual gift is an exciting endeavor. Once you uncover it, you will see the indispensable role you play.

CAREFUL ARRANGEMENT

Just like a human body is comprised of many parts, God arranges the members of each spiritual community just as he pleases (1 Corinthians 12:18). That means he carefully placed each believer in his or her local body of Christ.

That the Lord chose to place you among the believers in your church confronts the lie that can infiltrate your thoughts: *The people in this church are so different from me. I don't feel like I have much in common with them. I wonder if it's a mistake that I'm here.* If God used your spiritual community to reach you for Christ, you can be confident he planted you there.

Spiritual growth looks much like biological growth. God uses more than Scripture and prayer to develop our faith. He uses members of the body of Christ to nourish it. He arranges opportunities for us to serve that move us closer toward Christ-like maturity. This might explain why the Apostle Paul gives us a principle that each person "should continue to live in whatever situation the Lord has placed you and remain as you were when God first called you" and strongly adds, "This is my rule for all the churches" (1 Corinthians 7:17). If the Lord assigned you a place in a local body, you should remain "as you were when God first called you" unless he calls you elsewhere.

God may prompt you to find fellowship elsewhere for a variety of reasons. Nevertheless, you should examine your motives. Is pursuing money or career advancement the driving force in your decision? James explicitly criticizes this.

> Listen, you who say "Today or tomorrow we will go to this or that city, spend a year there, carry on business and make money." Why, you do not even know what will happen tomorrow… Instead, you ought to say, "If it is the Lord's will, we will live and do this or that" (James 4:13-15).

Disconnecting yourselves from community not only hampers your spiritual growth; it harms the body of Christ.

INTERCONNECTED

If one part of your body gets injured, it impacts everything else. For example, losing your leg in an accident would permanently change your life. Likewise, God arranged us in the body of Christ to support one another and meet each other's needs.

My family and I recently visited Sequoia National Park in Southern California. The giant sequoia redwoods are some of the biggest trees in the world. The park has the largest living tree, nicknamed "General Sherman." It stands 275 feet tall and has a girth of 105 feet.

You would expect that something this big would have an incredible root system that burrows deep into the ground. However, their roots only go down about 10 feet. Yet they rarely fall over. Despite their shallow root systems, these trees withstand strong winds, earthquakes, fires and prolonged flooding.

So how can a 2,000-year-old, 500-ton tree remain standing with roots that go down only 10 feet? They grow in clusters.

Beneath the surface are intertwining root systems that act like an army of men and women with interlocked arms, supporting each other. Much like a grove of giant sequoias, we provide stability and support for each other as the adversities of life threaten to knock us down. We help supply each other with vital nutrients as God causes the growth.

GROWTH

Healthy organisms grow. Well-watered trees in nutrient-rich environments flourish. Thriving newborns double their weight in the first six months. In the same way, a healthy body of Christ grows as "each part does its work."

You see, the Christian life isn't just about enjoying God's blessing. It's not purely a pursuit of peace and personal happiness. It cannot be reduced to enjoying intimacy with God. It's more than experiencing healing from past traumas. The Christian life is also about contributing to the overall health and growth of the body of Christ.

Indeed, our intimacy with God impels us to love others. Our merciful Father gives us peace, he changes our lives, he heals our wounds; he does so not only to fill our lives with joy, but to make us more effective at playing our part in building up the body of Christ.

Heavenly Father, thank you for placing me in such a wonderful fellowship. You say that it's good and pleasant for brothers and sisters to dwell together in unity. It's truly a privilege to be surrounded by believers who are eager to serve me and build up my faith in you. I can't imagine going through the hardships of life without the body of Christ. Lord, your sovereignty gives me confidence that you placed me here, at this time, for the purpose of playing my unique role. Help me play my small part in your larger plan of redeeming this broken world. In Jesus' name, Amen.

SEVENTEEN
Bride of Christ

For your Creator will be your husband; the LORD of Heaven's Armies is his name! He is your Redeemer, the Holy One of Israel, the God of all the earth.
ISAIAH 54:5 (NLT)

Husbands, love your wives, as Christ loved the church and gave himself up for her to make her holy, cleansing her by the washing with water through the word, and to present her to himself as a radiant church, without stain or wrinkle or any other blemish, but holy and blameless.
EPHESIANS 5:25-27

God uses marriage as a metaphor for our union with him. The New Testament sometimes calls Jesus the "bridegroom" and the church his "bride." For example, the book of Revelation depicts the reunion between Jesus and his followers as a wedding feast. John the Apostle beams us to the scene of a roaring multitude shouting:

"Let us rejoice and be glad and give him glory! For the wedding of the Lamb has come, and his bride has made herself ready. Fine linen, bright and clean, was given her to wear." (Fine linen stands for the righteous acts of God's holy people.) Then the angel said to me, "Write this: Blessed are those who are invited to the wedding supper of the Lamb!" (Revelation 19:7-9)

Depending on your background, you might see this metaphor through a certain filter. Collective societies tend to view the bride of Christ metaphor as a corporate identity, the church as a whole. Whereas cultures that prize individualism personalize it. They see this metaphor as a picture of intimacy individual believers enjoy with God. Scripture applies it both ways. Let's examine this metaphor from both angles.

OUR VIEW OF THE CHURCH

Each time the New Testament drapes the bride of Christ metaphor onto the church, it speaks of the church's purity. For example, the Apostle Paul pictures himself as the Corinthian church's father, offering his daughter to God as Christ's bride: "I am jealous for you with a godly jealousy. I promised you to one husband, to Christ, so that I might present you as a pure virgin to him" (2 Corinthians 11:2).

What God wants us to envision can be difficult to see. "On earth," Bible commentator John Stott observes, "[the church] is often in rags and tatters, stained and ugly, despised and persecuted. But one day she will be seen for what she is, nothing less than the bride of Christ, 'free from spots, wrinkles or any other disfigurement.'"[37] But Stott is talking about the church's radiant appearance at the wedding banquet of the Lamb.

We don't have to stare at our watches for Christ's return to view the church as blameless. Paul reminds the Colossian believers that Christ "reconciled you in His fleshly body through death, in order to present you before Him holy and blameless and beyond reproach" (Colossians 1:22). God views us as his unblemished bride, right now.

It's often difficult to see the church the way God sees it. It's easy to fixate on the church's blemishes and look at it with disdain. I once heard Christian author Jim Putman tell a story that highlighted the problem with holding the church in contempt. As a brand-new Christian, Putman told his dad that he wanted to follow Christ but didn't want to have anything to do with the church.

A few weeks later, his dad called him and said, "Hey, Jim, I want to get some advice. A family in the church invited me over for dinner, but they didn't invite Mom. I don't think they like Mom."

Furious, Putman said, "I get why they don't like you… But Mom?"

"What should I do?" his dad asked.

Putman replied, "There's no way. They can't invite you and not invite Mom. That's just not right."

His dad paused.

Putman said anytime his dad paused like this, it meant something just happened. His dad said, "Jim, that's how Jesus feels about his bride, the church. You can't say you love Jesus, but not his bride."

His dad continued, "The bride doesn't always look beautiful. She's a work in progress, and you should see your part in that."

If you choose to focus on the broken stuff in the church, you will find plenty of problems. It's true. The church has been wracked with financial and sex scandals. Many non-Christians regard Jesus' followers as hypocrites, a reputation that sadly is often deserved. But imperfect groups of Christians across the world are reaching people for Jesus, helping the poor and raising up disciples.

CULTIVATING INTIMACY

We can also apply the marriage metaphor to our personal interactions with God. An array of images fill our heads when we hear the word "marriage." Some connect it with scenes of Mom and Dad raising their voices at each other. For others, marriage stirs up images of parents living parallel lives. Despite some of the poor examples we've seen, God designed marriage to provide unequaled closeness with another person.

Scripture depicts marriage as two becoming "one flesh" (Genesis 2:24). Nothing defines intimacy more than uniting yourself to another and becoming one. In the same way, our faith in Christ binds us to God.

This union gives us unlimited access to God. The author of Hebrews describes the type of intimacy available to us as Christ's bride:

> Therefore, brothers and sisters, since we have confidence to enter the Most Holy Place by the blood of Jesus, by a new and living way opened for us through the curtain, that is, his body, and since we have a great priest over the house of God, let us draw near to God with a sincere heart and with the full assurance that faith brings, having our hearts sprinkled to cleanse us from a guilty conscience and having our bodies washed with pure water. (Hebrews 10:19-22)

We can turn to God at any time, with any request, without shame. God delights in us sharing our victories, expressing our gratitude and voicing our appreciation for him. He also encourages us to speak with honesty about our fears, doubts, anxieties, even our anger.

The Psalms provide us with uncomfortable examples of people expressing their emotions to God. The psalmists furnish us with their raw, unedited prayers. At times, the way they speak to the Lord borders on irreverence. Yet our Heavenly Father included them in Scripture to give us a pattern for pouring out our hearts to him.

God delights in us drawing near to him. He not only desires for us to fix our minds on the profound truths contained in Scripture; he also yearns for us to connect with him on an emotional level.

Recently, I was talking to a friend who expressed feeling discouraged by his inability to connect with God. He was newly married. So, I said to him, "You have been married to your wife for a couple months. You are happy with your marriage. And yet, you don't feel enraptured by every interaction with your wife. All your interactions take place within the context of love. When you ask about her day at work or when you share a funny story you heard, all these interactions count toward building closeness with your wife."

We should think of our union with God the same way. Not every encounter will leave your face shining like the sun. You shouldn't feel alarmed. You may go through brief stretches when you may not feel God's presence. Yet he's ever-present and eager to spend time with you. As you persevere during these dry periods with God, they still add up to meaningful interactions over time.

Lord, I feel overwhelmed by the love you show me and your church. I look in the mirror and see nothing worthy of your love. But your son Jesus' blood washed me clean and transformed the church into a radiant bride. I earnestly pray you will help me see the church as you see her — as your beloved bride. I pray you would increase my love for the church, to match the love you have for the church. I pray that you would teach me to develop a close relationship with you. I desire to have the intimacy Jesus enjoyed with you while he was on earth. Finally, help me to resist the world system's attempts to seduce me away from my affection to Christ. Amen.

EIGHTEEN
Temple of God

As you come to him, the living Stone — rejected by humans but chosen by God and precious to him — you also, like living stones, are being built into a spiritual house… For in Scripture it says: "See, I lay a stone in Zion, a chosen and precious cornerstone, and the one who trusts in him will never be put to shame."
1 PETER 2:4-6

The cornerstone was a crucial element of ancient construction. Experienced masons would select a premium stone from a quarry and hew it by hand. Once transported to the construction site, the cornerstone supported the building and set its dimensions. A master builder would place all other stones in reference to it. If the cornerstone was true, the building would be, too. If it was off, even slightly, the building would not be square.

In the same way, God set Jesus as the cornerstone of the church. He builds believers into a spiritual house in relationship to him. Jesus' teaching and example provide us with the dimensions for what things should look like. Quite literally, Jesus provides the plumb lines that define the church.

As Peter paints a picture of believers as a spiritual house, he makes several comparisons to one specific building — the Temple. The Temple area was the focal point of Jewish religious life in the first century A.D., a place where they would offer sacrifices and worship God together. It was still standing in Jerusalem as Peter wrote his letter, so he knew it would provide a provocative image for comparison. Though following God no longer revolved around the physical Temple, Peter saw it as symbolic of our function as Christ's community on earth.

WHAT WAS THE MAIN FUNCTION OF THE TEMPLE?

The Temple symbolized God's presence on earth. Of course, no building can contain an omnipresent being. Solomon acknowledged this before he built the first Temple in the 10th century B.C. "But will God really dwell on earth?" he asked in 1 Kings 8:27. "The heavens, even the highest heaven, cannot contain you. How much less this temple I have built!" The Lord never created the Temple with the intention of communicating it would house him. The Temple was proof of his willingness to meet us where we are.

The Temple acted as a type — an early visual example — of how God would enter human history through his son. The Apostle John tells us that Jesus "became flesh and made his dwelling among us" (John 1:14). John carefully chose the word "dwelling" because it pointed to the Temple. The symbol was God's presence in a building of stone; the reality was God living in a human body. That's why when Jesus said to the Pharisees, "Destroy this temple and I will raise it again in three days," John comments that "he was speaking of the Temple of his body" (John 2:19, 21).

After his death, resurrection and ascension, Jesus promised to send the Holy Spirit, who would make his dwelling in us. Jesus planned for his followers to serve as his replacement, since the church would act as God's visible presence on earth. This explains why Paul was able to ask the Corinthians, "Don't you know that you are a temple of God and that the Spirit of God dwells in you?" (1 Corinthians 3:16)

THE CHURCH ISN'T A PLACE, IT'S THE PEOPLE

Occasionally, a member in our fellowship will say to me, "I asked my friend to come to church today." I usually offer some encouragement, "That's great. I hope she takes up your offer." But I also explain, "We don't go to the church; we are the church." I take the extra step of explaining this distinction because it has profound implications for how we view the church.

As someone who grew up going to a very traditional church with liturgies, rituals and memorized prayers, this idea led to a complete paradigm shift. Even at a very young age, I wondered, *Why does God care if we perform rituals or recite memorized prayers?* It never made sense to me why God would care if I prayed to him in a cathedral or in my bedroom.

I remember the first time I heard a Bible teacher say, "The church isn't a place, it's the people of God." It confirmed my suspicion. An omnipresent God cannot be confined to a building. God takes up residence in our hearts. This means believers can access God at any time because we are the temple and the Spirit of God dwells in us.

As I said earlier, this fact contains several profound implications. Let's examine a few.

WE ARE TO BE DIFFERENT FROM THE WORLD

The Temple symbolized God's holiness. God used each element of the Temple, from the washbasin in the courtyard to the veil guarding the Most Holy Place, to express: "You and I, we are different. I am distinct from you. I am morally perfect, and you are morally corrupt." That's why he required the people to undergo elaborate rituals and washings before entering the Temple.

Now that we form God's temple, he displays his holiness through us.

This idea stands out as one of the main themes in 1 Peter. Peter was writing to believers under heavy persecution. One thing he drills into their heads is that they are to be holy or set apart from the rest of their culture. God calls on us to be different not only in moral conduct, but also in our values. Instead of living for money and possessions, reputation and power, he calls us to invest in things that will endure in the next life, such as our relationships and efforts to love people.

Our speech and conduct should set us apart from the world, too. Now, we shouldn't stand out for having a judgmental attitude toward our culture or for self-righteous moralizing. God wants us to stand out for the gratitude, joy and unity we share with other believers. That's why the Apostle Paul addressed the growing division among the Philippians by saying:

> Do everything without grumbling or arguing, so that you may become blameless and pure, "children of God without fault in a warped and crooked generation." Then you will shine among them like stars in the sky as you hold firmly to the word of life. (Philippians 2:14-16)

Our unity impacts more than just our relationships in the church; it impacts the way people view God.

AS LIVING STONES, WE'RE INTERCONNECTED

Many years ago, I traveled to Cusco, Peru, near the famous Incan citadel, Machu Picchu. During a tour of the city, our guide showed us a wall dating back to the 1,200s. The wall contained stones of various shapes and sizes, some of them triangular, which ancient masons dry fit together. The joints held so tight that our guide pulled out a blade and declared, "You can't even stick a knife edge between these stones."

As I ran my finger between the joints, the skill of these master craftsmen amazed me. This is the kind of connectedness God envisions for the church. The Lord took great care to place us exactly where he wants in his spiritual community, joining us with other believers to create a spiritual house.

To gain a deeper appreciation of this, it may be helpful to think about the opposite. Imagine you had a large pile of stones in your backyard. If someone snuck into your backyard and took one, you wouldn't notice.

Sadly, this picture fits the experience of many who attend church in America. The average Christian often feels like just another person in the crowd at the Sunday morning service. If she is struggling, she wouldn't know where to turn. If she stopped showing up, no one would notice.

This stands in sharp relief to the one God paints for us in Peter's letter. He sees the church as a beautiful arrangement of diverse, interrelated people who love and support each other.

GOD GIVES US A UNIQUE ROLE IN SUPPORTING OTHERS

In a wall, each stone supports the surrounding ones while also receiving support from them. If a stone were missing, you would notice right away. You would see a hole, and its absence would weaken the wall.

Similarly, a spiritual community pays the price when a member decides not to show up or refuses to contribute. The absence leaves a gap that impacts the rest of the church, since God gives each member a unique role in meeting others' needs.

The Apostle Paul uses the metaphor of a human body to illustrate the same concept.

> God has placed the parts in the body, every one of them, just as he wanted them to be… The eye cannot say to the hand, "I don't need you!" And the head cannot say to the feet, "I don't need you!" (1 Corinthians 12:18, 21)

Each part of your body plays an important role. If you injure one part, the rest suffers. Imagine if you lost an arm, a foot or an organ! In the same way, when a living stone is missing, it affects the entire structure because the master builder put it there for a purpose.

LIVING STONES ENJOY UNITY AND DIVERSITY

As God's temple, we become part of something bigger than ourselves. And yet, we remain individuals, each with unique qualities. The Lord positioned us in our spiritual community to play our role, with the spiritual gifts he has given us.

As a young Christian, I remember enjoying the unity I shared with other believers. I felt as if I belonged. Yet I also wrestled with how I could maintain my individuality. I came to realize: *The highest expression of individuality can be found only in community.*

It's easy to lose sight of the tremendous privilege we have as God's temple. We grumble about the amount of time we spend in community, feeling as if it's a heavy burden. We complain about certain members of the church, sometimes holding them in contempt. And yet, we fail to acknowledge that God placed us where he wanted us. God didn't make a mistake. He called you to serve, love and support those around you. And he placed those people around you to meet your spiritual needs and help you grow with him.

Lord, I am humbled that you choose to radiate your glory and presence through the church. It's a privilege to share the unity of the Spirit with other believers. I'm grateful that you have surrounded me with spiritual friends who love and care about me, especially when so many in our culture feel alone. I'm also grateful that I have a role to play in their lives as well. Help me never to lose sight of this great blessing. Amen.

NINETEEN
Royal Priesthood

As you come to him, the living Stone — rejected by humans but chosen by God and precious to him — you also, like living stones, are being built into a spiritual house to be a holy priesthood, offering spiritual sacrifices acceptable to God through Jesus Christ.
1 PETER 2:4-5

You are a chosen people, a royal priesthood, a holy nation, God's special possession, that you may declare the praises of him who called you out of darkness into his wonderful light.
1 PETER 2:9

The word "priest" calls to mind images of a person wearing an ornate robe performing rituals or someone who wears all black with a white tab collar. That's not what Scripture means when it refers to a priest. The New Testament picture of priesthood comes from the Old Testament. Therefore, we will examine what role priests played in God's covenant with Israel and then see how it relates to our new identity in Christ.

UNIQUE SERVICE FOR GOD

The nation of Israel relied on the priesthood to worship the Lord under the Old Covenant. Priests offered sacrifices, carried out rituals and ful-filled duties in the Temple, which symbolized God's presence on earth. Only priests could enter the Temple's main room, the Holy Place, and only the High Priest could enter the innermost room, called the Most Holy Place.

In the book of Exodus, God envisioned the entire nation of Israel serving as a holy nation and "a kingdom of priests" (Exodus 19:6). Each man and woman would play a unique role in representing God to the world and in helping others know him better. But God changed his plan when the Israelites disqualified themselves from his service.

As God was giving Moses the Law atop Mount Sinai, the Israelites grew impatient and demanded that Aaron, Moses' brother, make a god for them to worship. So Aaron took the jewelry plundered from Egypt and forged a golden calf. Sometime later, Moses descended Mount Sinai and burned with anger when he found the people worshipping an idol. At once, he called for the people's allegiance, and only the Levites responded (Exodus 32). Thus, God took the Levites and made them his priests (Numbers 8:18).

Jesus' death and resurrection ushered in a new way of relating to God without the need for a temple or sacrifices (John 4:23). And since God united us with Christ, who serves as our heavenly high priest, he made us into a royal priesthood. Thus, he fulfilled his promise to make for himself a kingdom of priests through the body of Christ.

CHOSEN BY GRACE

God not only gave the priesthood unique access to him, but he also gave them the privilege of serving in the Temple. He didn't choose them because of their moral fortitude. After all, the Levites worshipped the golden calf with the rest of Israel. The Lord chose them because of their willingness to repent.

Likewise, God chose you and me, not because we are something special, but because he's gracious. He made us into nation of royal priests, a chosen people (1 Peter 2:9-10). This new identity should motivate us to serve God. We shouldn't view it as burdensome or distasteful. Instead, we should see serving God as a great privilege we do with joy.

BOLD ACCESS TO GOD

The Temple was an earthly copy of a heavenly reality. It symbolized God's perfect moral character, and our unworthiness to approach him.

The Lord warned that no one could enter the Most Holy Place other than the chosen High Priest. Even he could enter only once a year on the Day of Atonement. God placed a physical barrier between the Holy Place and the Most Holy Place to signify the separation between himself and humans. A thick veil met anyone who intended to enter without the right credentials or at the wrong time. Furthermore, the High Priest had to offer sacrifices for his own sins and undergo a ritual cleansing before going beyond the veil (Leviticus 16:1-4).

All of this changed once God put the New Covenant in place. The author of Hebrews announces we can go past "the veil" and enter God's throne room at any time without concern about our guilt. What an amazing privilege. And it gets even better:

> Therefore, brothers and sisters, since we have confidence to enter the Most Holy Place by the blood of Jesus, by a new and living way opened for us through the curtain, that is, his body, and since we have a great priest over the house of God, let us draw near to God with a sincere heart and with the full assurance that faith brings, having our hearts sprinkled to cleanse us from a guilty conscience and having our bodies washed with pure water. (Hebrews 10:19-22)

Unlike the requirements for the High Priest to enter his presence, God does not make us offer a sacrifice for our sins or cleanse ourselves through ritual washing. He signed the New Covenant with Jesus' blood which washes away our moral guilt.

Shame from our past often hangs like a shroud when we approach God. Memories of failure flood our minds as we turn to him in prayer. They remind us of how unfit we are to come into his presence. In some cases, shame drives us to perform. We tell ourselves that if we can string together a few months of faithfulness, it will dispel the shame. For some of us, shame keeps us away from God altogether. In either case, we find ourselves cowering as we approach God.

Yet, Scripture declares that fear cannot survive in love: "Perfect love casts out fear" (1 John 4:18). To use Francis Schaeffer's term, God has taken away our "true moral guilt."[38] That means we can enter God's presence knowing he has cleansed us of our sins.

BUILDING GOD'S SPIRITUAL HOUSE

Peter tells us that God views us as a royal priesthood "offering spiritual sacrifices" in a "spiritual house." The construction of a spiritual house depicts God growing his church. Offering spiritual sacrifices means building up and serving others in the body of Christ. In God's plan, everyone plays a part.

Modern Western churches have strayed from the New Testament picture. Most have a lead pastor or a priest who seeks direction from God to guide the church. In some cases, he has an elder board of advisors, but it often lacks any decision-making authority. In larger congregations, the lead pastor hires an executive staff to carry out his directives. Paid staff are the ones who perform the "ministry" in the church.

Then you have everyone else who shows up to the weekly services. They come Sunday morning expecting to feel blessed by the worship and motivated by the pastor's sermon. Average members can participate in basic acts of service, such as landscaping church grounds or serving as an usher, but never in more sophisticated tasks of ministry such as teaching the Bible. Those are reserved for the professional minister, who has seminary training.

This distinction between trained pastor and typical member is foreign to the New Testament picture of the church. The Apostle Paul tells us that God "gave the apostles, the prophets, the evangelists, the pastors and teachers, to equip his people for works of service" (Ephesians 4:11-12). In other words, God raises up spiritual leaders and Bible teachers for the purpose of equipping members to serve within the church. The Lord also bestows spiritual gifts upon each of us the moment we come to Christ as we covered earlier.

NEW TESTAMENT WORSHIP

Priests facilitated worship in the Old Covenant. Now that God has instituted a New Covenant, what does it mean to worship?

To many Christians, worship means lifting our voices in praise to the Lord. Although singing is a form of worship, New Covenant practice entails much more than corporate singing. Scholar David Peterson argues:

> Contemporary Christians obscure the breadth and depth of the Bible's teaching on this subject when they persist in using the word "worship" in the usual, limited fashion, applying it mainly to what goes on in Sunday services.[39]

According to God, worship should find expression in everyday life.

For example, it takes place when we heap praise upon God and thank him for all he has done (Hebrews 13:15). This should take place not only during Sunday morning gatherings; it should also appear during times of personal prayer. Expressing gratitude gives us hope during trials. It aids our battle against intrusive thoughts. It gives us perspective as we struggle with difficult circumstances. And it shows our appreciation of who God is.

Another form of worship is generous giving. Paul describes the Philippians' financial help as "a fragrant offering, an acceptable sacrifice, pleasing to God" (Philippians 4:18). He uses Temple images, such as the fragrant offering, to show how financial generosity has taken the place of Old Testament rituals.

We also can worship God by sharing the message of Christ. Paul talks about his "priestly duty of proclaiming the gospel of God" in Romans 15:16. Paul uses the Greek word for "liturgy," a repeated series of prayers and rituals that priests would perform. Paul sees himself mimicking the Old Testament priests and understands his proclamation of the gospel as his "priestly duty."

Worship isn't something you do once a week while singing with other Christians. It's a way of life. Paul states this emphatically in Romans 12:1: "I urge you therefore, brethren, by the mercies of God, to present your bodies a living and holy sacrifice, well-pleasing to God, which is your spiritual service of worship." Placing your entire life on the altar of sacrifice is your greatest act of worship.

Lord, help me to see the privilege I have as your chosen royal priest. I pray I would take advantage of the unparalleled access I have to you. I pray I would serve you with eagerness and with my entire life in light of the mercies you have shown me. Amen.

TWENTY
Salt + Light

"You are the salt of the earth. But if the salt loses its saltiness, how can it be made salty again? It is no longer good for anything, except to be thrown out and trampled underfoot. You are the light of the world. A town built on a hill cannot be hidden. Neither do people light a lamp and put it under a bowl. Instead they put it on its stand, and it gives light to everyone in the house. In the same way, let your light shine before others, that they may see your good deeds and glorify your Father in heaven."

MATTHEW 5:13-16

Jesus uses an odd metaphor to describe the kind of life we should live before the watching world: "You are the salt of the earth." You might ask: *How is salt appealing?* Have you ever mistaken salt for sugar while baking? It's not pleasant.

Salt is a key element in savory foods. Salt turns up the volume of certain ingredients in a well-composed dish. Too little, and your food tastes bland. Too much, and it's inedible. Just the right amount creates balance. Salt intensifies flavor and allows ingredients to sing within a dish. In the same way, your good deeds enhance the gospel when you tutor a student from an impoverished neighborhood or check on an elderly neighbor during a heatwave (Titus 2:10).

Some take this too far, however. They suggest we do not have to declare the message of Christ. Instead, our lives alone should communicate God's love. They even quote a popular saying often attributed to St. Francis of Assisi: "Preach the gospel always, and if necessary, use words."

This saying does not fit with Jesus' command to bring the message of salvation to the ends of the earth (Acts 1:8). Paul explicitly states that faith comes through hearing the word of Christ.

> How, then, can they call on the one they have not believed in? And how can they believe in the one of whom they have not heard? And how can they hear without someone preaching to them? (Romans 10:14)

Salt is necessary to season your food, but you would never want a plate of it for dinner. In the same way, a believer's lifestyle should complement the wonderful message of the gospel — not replace it.

Salt was an important commodity in the ancient world. It not only seasoned food; it also preserved it. We live in an age of refrigeration, which keeps perishable food at safe temperatures, but food quickly spoiled in the ancient world. A small family would often have lots of meat left once they slaughtered a lamb or a calf from the herd. So they discovered ingenious ways to preserve food.

In Europe, people ground and encased meat in animal intestines, which protected it from bacteria. That's how we got sausage. Another popular technique was salt curing. You would encrust fish or beef in salt to draw out moisture and make it inhospitable to bacteria. This process led to the invention of wonderful foods such as bacon, cured ham, pastrami and jerky.

In the same way, God wants us to preserve the message of Christ by faithfully proclaiming the gospel.

The beauty of the gospel is its simplicity. Yet God's enemy relentlessly propagates false teaching and ideologies that dilute its potency. For example, universalism doesn't seek to contradict the good news of Jesus; it paints it as one of many ways to God. Some authors try to rehabilitate God's image in the modern world by questioning hell's existence. Instead of highlighting God's love and mercy, they undermine his justice and undervalue Jesus' sacrificial death.

God calls on his followers, to preserve the integrity of the gospel by faithfully sharing it with those who do not know Christ and by discerning ways his enemy may be subverting its power. The Lord entrusted this task to us: "God was reconciling the world to himself in Christ, not counting people's sins against them. And he has committed to us the message of reconciliation" (2 Corinthians 5:19).

Ancient people used salt for agricultural purposes, too. Unlike modern table salt, ancient salts contained nutrients useful for fertilizing soil. Other ancient cultures, such as the Chinese and the Romans, used salt as fertilizer. Ancient farmers would add salt to manure piles to prevent them from rotting and to enhance their fertilizing properties. This might explain why Jesus says, "You are the salt of the earth" in Matthew 5:13 and why he makes the comment in Luke 14:35: "It is fit neither for the soil nor for the manure pile; it is thrown out." Following Jesus' analogy, our lives can catalyze spiritual life and growth in God's kingdom.

Jesus warns us, however, that we can lose our saltiness: "But if the salt loses its saltiness, how can it be made salty again?" Israel has an abundance of salt because of the Dead Sea, which contains a higher salt content than the ocean. You can walk along and pick up large salt crusts that naturally form on its beaches. However, these salt deposits contain a lot of impurities. Since the salt is more soluble than the impurities, it could leach out, leaving a substance of little worth.[40] Likewise, our lives can lose attractiveness if they lack distinction from the world and its values or if the watching world can identify discrepancies between our words and our actions.

Jesus shifts analogies and compares our lives to the light from a lamp. Unlike our electrified modern world, you wouldn't see light pollution radiating from an ancient city. Blue light from screens did not illuminate ancient homes after dinnertime. Night was pitch black.

I never experienced this until I visited Mammoth Cave National Park, the world's longest known cave system with more than 400 miles explored. During the tour, the guide turned off her lamp. "Oohs" and "aahs" rang from the crowd. Children squealed with excitement. The darkness was disorienting. There was no visual difference between having your eyes open or closed. After a minute, quiet fell over the group. The guide instructed us to wave our hands in front of our faces. You could not sense your hand inches from your face. That immediately changed when the guide turned on her lamp.

Jesus looks directly at us and says, "You are the light of the world."

We live in a dark world, morally speaking. Many Western men and women walk around aimless and disoriented, groping through the darkness, desperately grasping for meaning and purpose. It's in this context that God calls us to shine. Our lives should accentuate the message of Christ (salt), and it should expose by contrast the darkness around us (light).

We can do this in two ways.

First, we illuminate people's thinking with truth. We shouldn't presume the world will observe our lives and draw the right conclusions about God. A non-Christian cannot infer the gospel. We need to explain that the kindness and love they see in us result from faith in Jesus. Second, our lives should provide light in a dark world. They should cause neighbors, coworkers and family members to scratch their heads.

Yet this raises an important question: In what sense should we be different?

Some teach that we should avoid moral contamination by separating ourselves from the evil in the world. Under this paradigm, sin spreads like a contagion, infecting believers with moral filth. Therefore, these teachers encourage believers to create a hedge of protection around themselves and their families by eschewing secular movies, music and television for Christian alternatives.

Yet Jesus tells us that we shouldn't remove ourselves from the world: "They are not of the world any more than I am of the world. My prayer is not that you take them out of the world but that you protect them from the evil one" (John 17:14-15). Jesus doesn't want us to retreat. He wants our light to shine.

Of course, we bring light into the darkness by avoiding things such as sexual immorality, intoxication and bitter jealousy. Yet God also makes us distinct from the world by our good deeds.

Instead of living for fleeting things, God commands us to live for others. He calls us to bear each other's burdens, uphold the rights of the oppressed, advocate for the marginalized and give generously to the poor. When neighbors, co-workers, friends and family members notice that we value people more than things — and others more than ourselves — it creates curiosity. And if people ask, we should be prepared to give an answer to the hope that we have in Jesus.

Lord, develop in us a hunger to see people come to know Christ. Transform our lives so that we will act like salt and light in the world. I pray that you would develop in us a hunger to serve and love others. Help our lives to stand out. Let our good deeds, as well as our words, cause people to glory in you. Amen.

TWENTY-ONE
Citizen of Heaven

Our citizenship is in heaven. And we eagerly await a Savior from
there, the Lord Jesus Christ.
PHILIPPIANS 3:20

For he has rescued us from the dominion of darkness and
brought us into the kingdom of the Son he loves, in whom we
have redemption, the forgiveness of sins.
COLOSSIANS 1:13-14

Our relationship with Christ grants us a new status. Receiving Christ
rescues us from one kingdom and transfers us to another. We're no longer citizens of this world because God naturalizes us as citizens of heav-
en. As a result, our new status confers several benefits.

SECURITY

Ancient cities recorded citizens' names in a registry. City officials would
blot names from it when people died. Some evidence suggests ancient
cities would remove a citizen's name if found guilty of a crime. In the
first century, persecutors would brand unwavering Christians "political

rebels" and strip them of their citizenship.[41] But Jesus offered something no earthly authority could take away: citizenship in God's everlasting kingdom.

Jesus promised those who overcome temptation, "I will never blot out his name from the book of life, but will acknowledge his name before my Father and his angels" (Revelation 3:5).

In many parts of the world, political unrest and civil war displace large populations. In 2016, Americans watched in horror as millions of Syrians flooded European borders seeking asylum. News outlets flashed ghastly images of bodies washed ashore. Desperation filled refugees as they sought to start a new life in a foreign land.

Jesus' promise of a heavenly home provides peace and security in a world filled with instability. The moment we come to Christ, God promises us permanent residence in heaven. And he will never revoke our status.

In America, many grow up moving from one city to another. I've met young people who never lived in one place for more than two years because a parent served in the military or pursued career opportunities.

This lack of fixedness has produced a variety of insecurities. Some hesitate to wade deeper into relationships; others cling to friends for fear of losing them. Still others never bother to build relationships because they feel a constant impulse to move. Their restlessness doesn't allow them to settle down.

Those in Christ have a future heavenly home with ultimate stability. The friendships we form with believers will endure into eternity. We get to keep our friends.

EQUALITY AMONG GOD'S PEOPLE

Heavenly citizenship provides us with unparalleled unity. In our day, race continues to divide. We see a widening gap between rich and poor.

Women and the elderly still face discrimination in the workplace. Yet Christ broke down the dividing wall separating people along racial, social and gender lines. In the book of Ephesians, Paul calls on non-Jewish believers to stop seeing themselves as second-class citizens in God's kingdom. "You Gentiles are no longer strangers and foreigners," he insists. "You are citizens along with all of God's holy people. You are members of God's family" (Ephesians 2:19).

At Dwell, our student groups enjoy a great deal of diversity. Young people from different socio-economic backgrounds, races and cultures meet weekly to share life. The first time I went on vacation with people from my fellowship, I roomed with a green-haired punk rocker from the suburbs. I listened in amazement, as if hearing strange sounds from a distant galaxy, when he played punk songs for me. I grew up on the streets listening to rap. We could not have been any more different. Yet he and I shared a level of unity I hadn't experienced with other people.

A PERMANENT DWELLING

God not only prepares a city for his people, but he also promises to give each person a permanent dwelling. Jesus said this to his disciples when he informed them of his departure:

> "My Father's house has many rooms; if that were not so, would I have told you that I am going there to prepare a place for you? And if I go and prepare a place for you, I will come back and take you to be with me that you also may be where I am." (John 14:2-3)

Modern Americans obsess over renovating their homes. They spend small fortunes to update their kitchens, clad their bathrooms with expensive stone or create serene landscapes. People in our culture choose custom finishes to put a stamp of individuality on their homes. They're attempting to create their own "slice of heaven."

As followers of Christ, we shouldn't attempt to construct permanent homes on earth. We forfeit our earthly possessions the moment we die.

Jesus tells us he's preparing a heavenly home for us. We can even infer that he's designing it to our specific tastes. God possesses intimate knowledge about us. He fashioned our personality and promises to give us the desires of our heart (Psalm 139:13). C. S. Lewis once said, "Your place in heaven will seem to be made for you and you alone, because you were made for it — made for it stitch by stitch as a glove is made for a hand."[42]

Indeed, God will spare no expense in the construction of your heavenly home. After all, "he did not spare even his own Son but gave him up for us all, won't he also give us everything else?" (Romans 8:32). Don't waste your time turning your earthly home into your permanent residence. God will construct a heavenly dwelling that will exceed your wildest dreams.

FUTURE HOPE

Finally, our heavenly citizenship offers comfort and rest. One thing that set apart the heroes of faith, who played such powerful roles in God's plan, was their longing for a heavenly homeland. Consider Abraham and Sarah's example:

> They did not receive what was promised, but they saw it all from a distance and welcomed it… If they had longed for the country they came from, they could have gone back. But they were looking for a better place, a heavenly homeland. That is why God is not ashamed to be called their God, for he has prepared a city for them. (Hebrews 11:13-16)

Nothing beats the feeling of coming home after a long flight or a grueling car ride. This longing increases the closer we get. What is it about home that brings us comfort and relief?

First, home represents a place where we can relax and unwind. In the same way, our heavenly home provides rest. In the Old Testament, Israel entered God's rest by occupying the Promised Land (Deuteronomy 25:19).

But God's rest extends way beyond this. It offers relief from the weight of sin. It ends our relentless pursuit of trying to earn God's favor. It frees us from fretting. In fact, Jesus soothed his disciples' fears about his departure by promising them a future dwelling place (John 14:1).

Second, our longing for home often seems connected to those awaiting us. Why does a devoted father rush home after a long day at work? It's because he longs to see his wife and children. Likewise, we feel growing anticipation to meet Jesus face to face as we approach the end of our lives. We eagerly await reuniting with friends and loved ones who went ahead of us to be with the Lord.

HERO'S WELCOME

Scripture assures us we will be greeted with a celebration when we arrive at our true place of residence. Imagine the reception we will receive when we finally go home to be with the Lord. Hebrews 12:1 reminds us that "We are surrounded by a great [throng] of witnesses," watching and cheering us on as we run our race. All of those we love who went before us, all of those we've impacted with the gospel, the heroes of faith we've studied and admired, the host of heaven and Jesus himself will rise to greet us with inexpressible joy as we come home. We will finally receive the praise and acknowledgement we've been looking for all our lives.

The elderly American missionary Samuel Morrison came home after serving for 25 years in Africa. He was traveling home on the same ocean liner that brought President Roosevelt back from a hunting expedition.

When the great ship pulled into the New York harbor, the dock was filled with what looked like the entire population of New York City. Bands were playing, banners were waving, flashbulbs were popping.

Roosevelt stepped down onto the gangplank and was greeted with thunderous applause and a shower of ticker tape. If the police had not restrained the crowd, they would have mobbed him.

At the same time, Morrison quietly walked off the boat. No one was there to greet him. He slipped through the crowd alone.

He later recounted how he began to complain, "Lord, the president has been in Africa for three weeks, killing animals, and the whole world turns out to welcome him home. I've given 25 years of my life in Africa, serving you, and no one has greeted me or even knows I'm here." In that moment, the Lord spoke to him and said,

"You're not home."

Lord, I long to be home with you. I am eager to see you face to face and to be transformed into your likeness. It's hard living in this fallen world. You know what it was like. I take comfort in knowing it is only temporary. Thank you that you let me enjoy aspects of my heavenly citizenship now. I pray the future hope of heaven would motivate me not to put down roots in this world and to serve you with all my heart. Amen.

TWENTY-TWO
Temporary Resident

Dear friends, I warn you as "temporary residents and foreigners" to keep away from worldly desires that wage war against your very souls. Be careful to live properly among your unbelieving neighbors. Then even if they accuse you of doing wrong, they will see your honorable behavior, and they will give honor to God when he judges the world.
1 PETER 2:11-12 (NLT)

My parents emigrated from the Philippines in the early 1970s, leaving behind many of their relatives. Throughout my childhood, aunts and uncles would come to visit from the Philippines, often staying with us for weeks or months at a time. They never attempted to assimilate into American culture during their stay. My relatives didn't alter the way they dressed unless it was a blustery Chicago winter. They sampled a variety of American dishes, but they mostly ate Filipino food. Why? My relatives planned on returning to their country.

Likewise, Peter peels our eyelids back to help us see that we're residing as foreigners on earth — simply passing through this world. The Apostle John takes it one step further. He tells us the world itself is passing away and warns us not to let our world's values seduce us away from God:

> Do not love this world nor the things it offers you… For the world offers only a craving for physical pleasure, a craving for everything we see, and pride in our achievements and possessions. These are not from the Father, but are from this world. And this world is fading away, along with everything that people crave. (1 John 2:15-17)

The "world" refers to the system of values that stands opposed to God. John pleads with us to resist its overtures since the "world is fading away."

Unlike most people today, the citizens of our heavenly home will not organize their lives around sensuality, the pursuit of soulless materialism or success-inflamed egotism. Two values will tower above all others in our heavenly country: loving God and loving people. The citizens of heaven will absorb themselves in finding new ways to enhance these relationships.

After all, these will be the only things left standing after Christ's return. The Apostle Peter warns:

> But the day of the Lord will come like a thief. The heavens will disappear with a roar; the elements will be destroyed by fire, and the earth and everything in it will be laid bare. Since everything will be destroyed in this way… You ought to live holy and godly lives as you look forward to the day of God and speed its coming. (2 Peter 3:10-12)

Living as a temporary resident in a foreign land not only entails a certain lifestyle; it also presents unique challenges.

PEOPLE TEND TO WATCH FOREIGNERS CLOSELY

We often view foreign people's behavior as odd because it's different. Several years ago, members of our Nepali refugee ministry celebrated a special occasion by slaughtering a chicken on the sidewalk near the main entrance of our building. I remember the look of horror on people's faces as they filed into the parking lot after the morning service.

Likewise, people look upon radical commitment to Christ as odd. This pattern dates back to ancient times. As Christianity exploded in the Roman world, accusations began swirling. During the second century A.D., people accused Christians of a variety of crimes including cannibalism and incest.[43] Of course, it's not hard to imagine. Married couples referred to each other as "brother" and "sister," and non-Christians heard believers talking about communion where they ate Christ's body and drank his blood.

Today, groups of Christians often come under greater scrutiny if they are making a major impact on a city or within a community. People fear and distrust what they don't understand. A new believer's friends and family may not like all the changes they see. Parents furrow their brows when they see their son or daughter suddenly prioritize God over other things in life. Friends shake their heads when they no longer take interest in drunken partying or getting high. Neighbors scratch their heads when they see a follower of Jesus live below her means to give more. Coworkers raise questions about a believer's sanity when he walks away from a promising career because it interferes with his commitment to his family and serving Christ.

FOREIGN PEOPLE OFTEN FACE MOCKERY AND REJECTION

Noah attracted odd looks during his day. God tells us, "Noah was a righteous man, blameless among the people of his time, and he walked faithfully with God" (Genesis 6:9). This meant Noah lived to please God. He had integrity. The reason he could be "righteous" and the reason he could be "blameless" had to do with his walk with God. Of course, Noah wasn't perfect. However, Noah walked with God. That meant he made decisions about his life based on his relationship with God.

Don't forget context. Moses tells us, "The LORD saw how great the wickedness of the human race had become on the earth, and that every inclination of the thoughts of the human heart was only evil all the time" (Genesis 6:5). Noah was living for God when no one else was. He was marching out of step with the culture because he was walking with God.

Noah's neighbors saw him as an eccentric. They thought he was crazy because he wasn't conforming to the culture. Noah didn't believe something just because everyone else believed it. He didn't do things just because everybody else did. He sought to please God, not people.

When you live in a world like his, there's a lot of pressure. Some of you live and work in pressured environments. You're being squeezed. Some of you are in educational institutions that are pressing in on you because your values are at odds with your culture. As our society becomes more post-Christian, the more serious you get about your walk with God, the odder you will look.

One day, God warned Noah about a catastrophic flood he would send on the land for the people's evil deeds. He instructs Noah to build an ark, a flat-bottomed boat made of gopher wood.

Can you imagine the ridicule you would face building an enormous boat in the middle of the desert? Your neighbor comes out of her house and asks, "What are you working on?" You respond, "A barge. God told me he would send a worldwide flood to destroy all life on earth." She raises her eyebrows and asks with a slight chuckle, "A flood?"

Noah must've endured this for years as he built the ark. His neighbors walk by his property. "How's the boat coming along? Did you hear the forecast?" they snicker. "Cloudy, with a chance of worldwide flood."

The Apostle Peter sheds further light on Noah's life. "If [God] did not spare the ancient world when he brought the flood on its ungodly people, but protected Noah, a preacher of righteousness, and seven others... then the Lord knows how to rescue godly men from trials" (2 Peter 2:5, 9).

He was a preacher of righteousness. I've always pictured Noah as this eccentric recluse, mumbling to himself in the desert. Instead, he was warning people about God's coming judgment. Noah chopped down trees during the day and then he preached at night. He was armed with a three-word sermon, "It's gonna rain. It's gonna rain."

The people were like, "What's rain?"

He says, "I don't know, but God is going to send it."

Talk about looking like a fool.

Put yourself in Noah's position. God warns you he will send a worldwide flood as judgment upon human evil. Year after year, decade after decade, you construct a boat that will save you and your family. And your faith in God is an object of derision among your neighbors. Then one day, you feel a rain drop.

OUR RESPONSE

As citizens of heaven passing through the world, we're going to stand out. But we should do so for the right reasons. Peter advises his audience to remove any valid accusations that were drawing negative attention: "Keep away from worldly desires that wage war against your very souls. Be careful to live properly among your unbelieving neighbors" (1 Peter 2:11-12). Peter uses a Greek word for "keep away," which often refers to maintaining control over one's appetites and desires. This word appeared in Greek ethical writing because the moral philosophers held self-control as a virtue.[44] Thus, Peter entreats his audience to maintain — at minimum — his culture's standard of moral conduct.

However, Peter wasn't suggesting a way out of suffering. He wanted their conduct to lead people into genuine faith in Christ: "Even if they accuse you of doing wrong, they will see your honorable behavior, and they will give honor to God when he judges the world" (1 Peter 2:12).

As false accusations about the church swirled in the ancient world, people could not ignore its good deeds. The Roman emperor, Julian the Apostate, who inflicted the church with punishing persecution in the 300s A.D., wrote:

> Why do we not observe that it is [the Christians'] benevolence to strangers, their care for the graves of the dead, and the pretended holiness of their lives that have done most to increase atheism [unbelief of the pagan gods]? ...For it is disgraceful that, when no Jew ever has to beg, and the impious Galileans [Christians] support not only their own poor but ours as well, all men see that our people lack aid from us.[45]

Even though rumors circulated about Christians in the early church, the watching world could not deny the love they expressed in caring for the poor. Jesus' love eventually won over most of the known world.

People in your city may say awful and slanderous things about Christians or about your church, but let your good deeds silence the ignorant talk of foolish men. Make sure you live in such a way that people will have to harmonize any negative thing they've heard about Christians with what they see in your life.

Lord, may we never grow discouraged as we face rejection for sharing the message of Christ and living radically for you. I pray that we would neither retaliate nor retreat. Instead, help us to live in such a way that causes people to scratch their heads and marvel at the love we radiate. Amen.

TWENTY-THREE
Ambassador

God was in Christ reconciling the world to Himself, not counting
their trespasses against them, and He has committed to us
the word of reconciliation. Therefore, we are ambassadors
for Christ, as though God were making an appeal through
us; we beg you on behalf of Christ, be reconciled to God.
2 CORINTHIANS 5:19-20

Ancient ambassadors functioned much like they do today. They were foreign diplomats who spoke on behalf of the nation or king they represented. Great royal houses often sent ambassadors to forge alliances with surrounding nations. In times of war, a conquering king would send an ambassador to negotiate the defeated king's surrender and secure a treaty.

In the same way, God appoints us to negotiate the terms of peace between him and those who stand in opposition. It's as if God was making his appeal to the world through us, "We beg you on behalf of Christ, be reconciled to God."

MINISTRY OF RECONCILIATION

God sees sin as an act of hostility. He considers any sin an act of rebellion since he's the rightful ruler of the universe. Thus, our true moral guilt puts us at odds with God. And yet,

> God demonstrates His own love toward us, in that while we were yet sinners, Christ died for us…For if while we were enemies we were reconciled to God through the death of His Son, much more, having been reconciled, we shall be saved by His life. (Romans 5:9,11)

Once we admit our guilt and accept his offer, God accepts us with open arms.

That's not all. Almighty God appoints us to be his ambassadors. He sends us into the world to represent his interests and share his message of reconciliation. We act as his mouthpiece to those who remain his enemies, communicating his terms of peace.

KNOWLEDGE OF CUSTOMS AND CULTURE

Today's ambassadors typically live in the country where they have been sent. This helps them obtain a high degree of fluency in the country's language — expanding their vocabulary and exposing them to local expressions. This enables them to communicate with clarity and tact. Ambassadors also strive to become experts of the country's history and culture. They discover nuances that you will never get from a book.

In the same way, Christians should understand the surrounding culture. Many American believers come across as out of touch and anticultural. But the Bible urges us to understand our culture — not just at the surface level. Scripture calls us to discern the thoughts underlying what we see. This enables us to communicate the message of Christ with effectiveness.

Before stepping onto one of the biggest intellectual stages of the ancient world, the Areopagus, Paul spent some time walking through the city of Athens (Acts 17). He observed Athenian culture and scoured Greek literature for points of contact with God's message of reconciliation. This influenced the direction of his discourse. Paul opens by pointing to an altar he found dedicated to an "Unknown God." He uses it as a launch pad to introduce his listeners to the one true God. He even quotes the Greek poets Aratus and Epimenides to relate with his audience.

If modern Christians want to remain relevant to a world in desperate need of God, we need to become students of culture. We need to see the philosophical underpinnings that animate cultural trends. We should be prepared to offer incisive critiques of these worldviews. However, we need to season our words with empathy. We shouldn't scoff at our culture. We should weep over its brokenness. We should exhibit the same compassion Jesus showed for the world as he wept over Jerusalem because they were like sheep without a shepherd (Matthew 9:36).

REPRESENTING IN WORD AND DEED

An ambassador doesn't speak on his own authority. He isn't allowed to express his personal opinions; he's not allowed to negotiate things for himself. He speaks on behalf of the country he represents. That's why Peter exhorts his audience as temporary residents in a foreign land, "If anyone speaks, he should do it as one speaking the very words of God" (1 Peter 4:11).

This means you should represent Christ in the way you speak, either in person or behind a keyboard. People keep a close eye on you once they find out you're a Christian. Even though you may separate your careless speech or strong opinions from people's impression of Christ, the world won't.

This also applies to the way you act. You might be familiar with the term

"Ugly American," which comes from Eugene Burdick's 1958 novel about American ambassadors in Southeast Asia after World War II. These ambassadors showed cultural insensitivity. Their behavior discredited America and thwarted our foreign policy. Today people use the term to describe the loud, obtuse, ethnocentric behavior of Americans traveling abroad. Ugly Americans disgrace their country because they're too self-absorbed to see how their behavior reflects poorly on their country.

Similarly, we can be "Ugly Christians." The world contains people searching for truth, who wonder if Jesus was who he claimed to be. They form their conclusions about Jesus largely by watching Christians, whether we like it or not.[46]

Paul showed a keen awareness of this. He was scrupulous not to hurt Christ's reputation — that his "ministry [might] not be discredited" (2 Corinthians 6:3).

We need to recover this sensitivity. One of the biggest hurdles facing people coming to Christ happens to be Christians. People will continue to hold a negative view of Christians until they meet believers who attract attention for their authenticity, love and unflappable confidence in Christ.

Consider how you represent Jesus to the world. Do coworkers hold you in high regard? Do people see you as friendly? Honest? Hardworking? Cooperative? Do you resist joining your coworkers as they complain and gossip about others at work? Do you have a good reputation with your neighbors? Are you hospitable? Are you helpful? How would your classmates describe you? Are you a distraction to other students? Are you likeable? Do they even know you follow Jesus?

These questions aren't meant to discourage or make you feel guilty. They're intended to help you see ways in which you can improve how you represent Christ.

THE URGENCY OF OUR TASK

Envoys have precious little time to reach a peace agreement. A breakdown in negotiations could result in hundreds of lives lost. This means ambassadors must convey the king's message with clarity and persuasive force.

The urgency of our mission is even more grave. Those who never lay down their arms and make peace with God will perish for the rest of eternity. Therefore, we must plead with them to reconcile with God. Christian author Watchman Nee expresses the urgency of our task with unusual force:

> Oh, that we might awaken to the weightiness of our responsibility, the urgency of the need around us, and the fleeting nature of time! … Our time is almost gone; the need is still desperate; our solemn obligation is still undischarged. Let us, as dying men, give ourselves with all our powers to the dying around us.[47]

This is not our home. One day we will be home in our heavenly dwelling, and our mission will be over. We have a one-of-a-kind opportunity to impact eternity.

Don't hold back anything. Don't keep anything in reserve. Empty yourself in service to God. We have another life ahead of us that will span eternity. This is the only life we can give in exchange for the lives of others.

Lord, you give us an incredible privilege of serving as your ambassadors in this world. Instruct and transform us so that we may represent you accurately to the people we encounter. Finally, I pray that you would build in us a fiery passion to share your message of reconciliation with clarity and urgency. Amen.

TWENTY-FOUR
Not of This World

May I never boast except in the cross of our Lord Jesus Christ, through which the world has been crucified to me, and I to the world.
GALATIANS 6:14 (NET)

"The world has hated them, because they are not of the world, even as I am not of the world. I do not ask You to take them out of the world, but to keep them from the evil one. They are not of the world, even as I am not of the world."
JOHN 17:14-16 (NASB)

"If the world hates you, keep in mind that it hated me first. If you belonged to the world, it would love you as its own. As it is, you do not belong to the world, but I have chosen you out of the world. That is why the world hates you. Remember what I told you: 'A servant is not greater than his master.' If they persecuted me, they will persecute you also."
JOHN 15:18-20

Dear friends, do not be surprised at the fiery ordeal that has come on you to test you, as though something strange were happening to you. But rejoice inasmuch as you participate in the sufferings of Christ, so that you may be overjoyed when his glory is revealed. If you are insulted because of the name of Christ, you are blessed, for the Spirit of glory and of God rests on you.
1 PETER 4:12-14

Modern people have come to demand a life that is comfortable, low-stress and pain-free. That's why many followers of Jesus feel as if someone sucker punched them when tragedy strikes. It's why some new believers feel disoriented when adversity reappears. They sought refuge in Jesus and thought hardships would disappear after they found him.

But Jesus never sugar-glazed what it would take to follow him. He told us up front that we will face opposition for our association with him. He didn't want us to feel blindsided when people mock us or sneer at our faith.

Jesus gives us a theological reason for it, too. We will experience hatred because we are "not of the world" even as he was not of the world (John 17:16). He chose us out of the world.

IN THE WORLD

The Greek word for "world" means more than our spinning blue globe making its way around the sun or the human civilizations occupying it. Biblical writers also used it to signify everything in the world that is hostile toward God and his purposes. The Apostle John describes the world as a system of values that God's enemy, Satan, uses to ensnare and distract us from God's purposes.

Complete escape from the world is impossible. The most extreme forms of self-denial "lack any value in restraining sensual indulgence" (Colossian 2:23). No amount of simple living will contain our desire to possess what we see. Even if we ran off to a monastery nestled in the mountains, pride in our moral achievements would find us.

Knowing this, Jesus never planned for his followers to withdraw fully from the world. Instead, he prayed to the Father: "I do not ask You to take them out of the world, but to keep them from the evil one" (John 17:15).

Escape from the world doesn't occur through grunting self-discipline or grimacing self-denial. Instead, escape comes through our identity in Jesus. We are not of the world because Jesus is not of the world. God liberated us when he united us with Christ. This is what enabled Paul to declare: "May I never boast except in the cross of our Lord Jesus Christ, through which the world has been crucified to me, and I to the world" (Galatians 6:14, NET).

NOT OF THE WORLD

We live in tension. We no longer belong to this world. Yet we live in it. The world hates Jesus for who he is and what he represents — a narrow passageway to God paved with humility. We are guilty by association.

Jesus suffered humiliation and shame though he was innocent. Should we expect better treatment? Let me make this clear: You will face persecution if you are a committed follower of Jesus. The sooner you accept this, the better off you will be. To be forewarned is to be forearmed.

Experts estimate that the force of a pro football player tackling you is the same as crashing your car into a brick wall at 30 miles per hour. The worst collisions usually take place when a player doesn't see it coming. If the player anticipates the tackle, it gives him a chance to brace for impact. These crucial milliseconds can be the difference between a player walking off the field or medical staff carting him off on a stretcher. Likewise, Peter warns believers: "Do not be surprised at the fiery ordeal that has come on you to test you, as though something strange were happening to you" (1 Peter 4:12).

The mere mention of "Christianity" or "Jesus" may arouse a negative response from some people. In these cases, it's clear we are being insulted because of the name of Christ.

It's not so clear in other cases. Sometimes we face hostility from the world due to the impact the gospel has on people and society. This was not uncommon in the New Testament church. The disciples not only endured insults, public shame and beatings for their belief in Jesus; they also met opposition due to the socio-economic impact of the gospel. For example, Luke tells us in the book of Acts:

> A silversmith named Demetrius, who made silver shrines of Artemis, brought in a lot of business for the craftsmen there. He called them together, along with the workers in related trades, and said: "You know, my friends, that we receive a good income from this business. And you see and hear how this fellow Paul has convinced and led astray large numbers of people here in Ephesus… There is danger not only that our trade will lose its good name, but also that the temple of the great goddess Artemis will be discredited." (Acts 19:24-27)

Previously, Paul freed a slave girl from an evil spirit who gave her the ability to see the future. This brought her owners a great deal of money. The young girl's owners seized Paul when their hope of making money was gone. They told the city magistrate, "These men are Jews, and are throwing our city into an uproar by advocating customs unlawful for us Romans to accept or practice" (Acts 16:20-21).

Greco-Roman society tolerated many religions, much like 21st-century America. The empire welcomed new beliefs so long as they did not disturb the social order. Roman society judged a worldview by whether it conformed to the values that held the empire together. Anything that undermined them was a threat.

Many modern people view Christian teaching as a threat to Western values. Followers of Jesus face hostility not just because of their loyalty to him, but also because of the Bible's stance on social issues. There's a growing consensus that Christian teaching is merely a tool that power structures use to reinforce oppression and bigotry.[48] The church faces growing antipathy because Scripture takes a countercultural stance on sexuality and gender. Just like the New Testament church, the modern church faces tremendous pressure to conform.

Jesus tells us something wonderful in John 15:15: "I have called you friends, for all things that I have heard from My Father I have made known to you." We like that part. Jesus is our friend. But three verses later, he says, "If the world hates you, keep in mind that it hated me first" (John 15:18). We don't like that part. But Jesus makes our choice clear. "You want to be my friend?" Jesus says, "That's great. But it comes with people hating you because of your connection to me."

Some followers of Jesus want people to like them at all costs. If that's your goal in life, then you are following the wrong person.

If you choose to serve Jesus, you may face insults, scorn, even a hit to your reputation. You must decide. Will you live for other people's praise? Or will you live for God's approval? It's one or the other. Paul expresses this in stark terms.

> Am I now trying to win the approval of human beings, or of God? Or am I trying to please people? If I were still trying to please people, I would not be a servant of Christ. (Galatians 1:10)

You can't please everyone. If Jesus couldn't please the people he tried to serve, you and I don't stand a chance.

Years ago, a concert pianist delivered a flawless performance at Carnegie Hall. After playing the last note of his piece, the crowd exploded with roaring applause. The conductor came over and commended the young man for his brilliant performance. But he noticed the pianist's face remained expressionless, unmoved by the standing ovation. The young man narrowed his eyes as if he saw something unusual.

"What's wrong?" the conductor said.

The young man motioned with his head to someone sitting in the front row. "He's not standing."

"Who?" the conductor asked.

The young man replied, "My teacher."

If we are living for God's approval, the one whose opinion matters, we won't care what others think. People's opinions of us will fade into our periphery as we "fix our eyes on Jesus, the author and perfector of our faith" (Hebrews 12:2, NASB).

Wouldn't it simplify your life if you lived only for God's approval? We are ultimately not responsible for how people react to us. If God approves, you can be confident that you are doing the right thing.[49]

Lord, you never call on us to do something you were unwilling to do yourself. I'm grateful that you sent your son, Jesus, to model for us what it looks like to live in this state of tension of being in the world and yet not belonging to the world. I pray that we can emulate his compassion for those who hated him. And I pray our hearts would never grow cold to the world even as it moves further away from you. Amen.

TWENTY-FIVE
Servant of Christ

'"Even on my servants, both men and women,
I will pour out my Spirit in those days."'
ACTS 2:18

"Whoever serves me must follow me; and
where I am, my servant also will be. My Father
will honor the one who serves me."
JOHN 12:26

Over the years, I've encountered people who've said, "I tried Christianity, and it just didn't work. It wasn't for me." They left the church and never looked back.

Of course, there are various reasons why people leave. Some grew up in Christian homes and felt as if their parents rammed the Bible down their throats. Others express feeling like following God wasn't fulfilling. They viewed their experience through the eyes of a consumer. They attended Sunday morning services asking, *What am I getting out of this? Is this church meeting my needs?*

This misses the point of the Christian life. God tells us true happiness and fulfillment come from serving and meeting others' needs. Every believer needs encouragement, love and support — but the focus should be on what we can give, not what we can take.

After Jesus performed the job of a household servant and washed his disciples' feet, he spoke to them:

> "Now that I, your Lord and Teacher, have washed your feet, you also should wash one another's feet. I have set you an example that you should do as I have done for you. Very truly I tell you, no servant is greater than his master… Now that you know these things, you will be blessed if you do them." (John 13:15-17)

John the Apostle uses the Greek word *makarios*, which most Bibles translate "blessed." But when you say that someone is blessed, most of the time you mean they're fortunate or lucky. *Makarios* can also mean "happy." This makes more sense in the context of Jesus washing his disciples' feet. Serving others in love will not make you more fortunate, but it will make you happier.

Society says that if you want to experience happiness, you need to love yourself. Scripture asserts the opposite.

If you want to experience true happiness, the key isn't to love yourself more. The key is to love *others* more. For example, the Apostle Paul exhorts believers to take their eyes off of self and place them onto others. "In humility," he writes, "value others above yourselves, not looking to your own interests but each of you to the interests of the others" (Philippians 2:3). Thinking of others more results in greater love for them: "Be devoted to one another in love. Honor one another above yourselves" (Romans 12:10).

But you might ask, "How can you love others if you don't love yourself?" The Apostle John offers this explanation.

> Dear friends, let us love one another, for love comes from God… This is how God showed his love among us: He sent his one and only Son into the world that we might live through him. This is

love: not that we loved God, but that he loved us and sent his
Son as an atoning sacrifice for our sins. Dear friends, since God
so loved us, we also ought to love one another. (1 John 4:7-11)

Since God poured his love into our hearts through Jesus, he gives us a unique basis to love others. God promises to meet our deepest needs — our longings for love and significance. He also assures us that he will take care of our basic needs as a loving father. This frees us to think of ourselves less and others more. It allows us to give ourselves without reservation or expectation.

Jesus was "a man of sorrows and familiar with suffering," but his life wasn't characterized by unhappiness (Isaiah 53:3). His own statement that those who serve will be happy suggests that his life was filled with joy. Jesus embodied self-sacrificial love. Unlike our definition of happiness, which largely hinges on circumstances and material wealth, Jesus tied his well-being to the love and significance his Father provided him. Jesus' secure position within the Godhead allowed him to give freely. It's in God's very nature to serve, and since he formed us in his image, it's part of our original design to serve. This is why we're happiest when we serve others.

NOT QUALIFIED TO SERVE?

Over the years, I've met believers from traditional church backgrounds who feel inadequate to serve God because they don't have formal theological training. In their minds, the trained professional "minister" performs ministry in the church. Yet we search Scripture in vain for passages to support this notion that you need formal training to serve God.

The New Testament provides us with a radically different picture of the way Jesus equipped his disciples. He opted for more hands-on training. After Jesus was baptized and the Holy Spirit descended upon him, he began his ministry by joining John the Baptist in baptizing people. His popularity immediately soared, and he "was gaining and baptizing more disciples than John" (John 4:1). The Apostle John immediately adds, "although in fact it was not Jesus who baptized, but his disciples" (John 4:2). We see the same thing when Jesus fed the multitudes with bread and fish. Matthew's gospel throws in that Jesus "gave the bread to the disciples, who distributed it to the people" (14:19).

These examples illustrate that Jesus called his disciples to engage in ministry from day one. You cannot learn how to serve God in a classroom. You need real-world experience. Christian author and professor Robert Coleman makes this observation in his influential work, *The Master Plan of Evangelism*:

> Jesus had no formal school, no Seminaries, no outlined course of study, no periodic membership classes in which He enrolled His followers. None of these highly organized procedures considered so necessary today entered at all into His ministry.[50]

By no means am I diminishing the importance of equipping people. Scripture frequently teaches the importance of learning biblical truth for serving God (2 Timothy 3:16-17). That does not mean, however, that you must be a scholar before you step out to love others.

Scripture supplies us with an abundance of passages that call the average believer to serve. The Apostle Paul addressed the book of Ephesians to all the believers in the city, not just the leaders. He affirms that God outfits everyone to contribute in "the work of service, so that the body of Christ may be built up" (Ephesians 4:12). In another letter, Paul tells the Corinthians that God assigns spiritual gifts to each believer for the common good (1 Corinthians 12:7). Of these gifts, Paul lists the gift of teaching and the prophetic gift of preaching. Contrary to this, the modern church reserves these roles for ministers with a seminary degree.

Don't wait to serve Christ until you feel qualified. You will never be adequate to change people's lives. It takes nothing less than the power of God to accomplish this, and that's available to any believer who wants it. Paul clearly understood this when he wrote:

We are confident of all this because of our great trust in God through Christ. It is not that we think we are qualified to do anything on our own. Our qualification comes from God. He has enabled us to be ministers of his new covenant. (2 Corinthians 3:4-6)

So how do you get started? What does this look like practically? For starters, you can serve others in the body of Christ by offering encouragement to someone who seems discouraged (1 Thessalonians 5:14). You can bear another believer's burdens through simple acts of service or listening when she expresses feeling overwhelmed with life (Galatians 6:2). You can share Jesus with friends and family. You don't need to know sophisticated arguments for the existence of God before you try. Paul proclaimed that Jesus is the Son of God days after his conversion. Just tell them how you met Christ and how God has changed your life.

Consider the blind man whom Jesus healed. He gave a simple explanation for his belief when the religious leaders pressed him to testify that Jesus broke the Sabbath. "Whether he is a sinner or not, I don't know," the man said. "One thing I do know. I was blind but now I see!" (John 9:25).

THE COST OF SERVING CHRIST

Once you get a taste of the joy that comes from making an impact for Christ, you have a choice. Will you devote your entire life to his service? Or will you serve him when it's comfortable or convenient? Serving God can be exhilarating. It's hard to put into words how it feels to hear someone you've been sharing Christ with for years tell you she just invited Jesus into her heart. The satisfaction of hearing a child you tutor from a low-income neighborhood express gratitude can fill your eyes with tears.

But serving Christ isn't always exciting. It can be hard and thankless work. This is why many say, "I didn't sign up for this. I'm volunteering my time. I'm not getting paid for this." Those who react this way have failed to count the cost. Jesus said that whoever wants to serve him must deny himself and take up his cross daily. And then he gives this illustration:

> "For who would begin construction of a building without first calculating the cost to see if there is enough money to finish it? Otherwise, you might complete only the foundation before running out of money, and then everyone would laugh at you. They would say, 'There's the person who started that building and couldn't afford to finish it!' Or what king would go to war against another king without first sitting down with his counselors to discuss whether his army of 10,000 could defeat the 20,000 soldiers marching against him? And if he can't, he will send a delegation to discuss terms of peace while the enemy is still far away." (Luke 14:28-33)

You will never know the full benefits of following Jesus unless you commit your entire life to him. Although serving Christ may at times leave you feeling tired or frustrated or with a little less in your bank account, it's always worth it. God has given you an opportunity to invest your most valuable resources to shape the landscape of eternity. You can take your money, which you would otherwise leave behind when you die, and finance projects that impact people spiritually and materially. And your return on investment would leave any investor in a state of disbelief. You can redeem your time, the only non-renewable resource you have, toward something meaningful beyond this life. You can convert that which is perishable into what will be imperishable. But as Jesus said, you need to count the cost.

Giving your life to God is weighty. Do not make this decision in haste. God wants you to identify potential failure points in your service to him. Will the thirst for your parents' approval determine your commitment to Christ? Or are you willing to endure disapproval to further God's purposes in the world? Is your pursuit of wealth on a collision course with your ambition to serve? Jesus makes it clear: You cannot serve both God and money (Matthew 6:24).

Are you willing to hand over these areas of your life and devote yourself to him? Do you believe that if you trust in the Lord, he will give you the desires of your heart? God has proven faithful time and again. Offer yourself to God as a living and holy sacrifice.

If you choose to dedicate your life to God, it will be filled with joy. However, this is the first of many decisions. As one author puts it, "The problem with living sacrifices is that they tend to crawl off the altar."

Lord, I'm grateful and humbled that you would use someone like me to carry out the important and urgent work of building up your church and sharing the good news of Jesus. Thank you that my adequacy to serve comes from Christ. I pray that you would change the course of eternity through the work I do for you in this life. Amen.

TWENTY-SIX
Combatant: Freedom Fighter

For though we live as human beings, we do not wage war according to human standards. For the weapons of our warfare are not human weapons, but are made powerful by God for tearing down strongholds. We tear down arguments and every arrogant obstacle that is raised up against the knowledge of God.
2 CORINTHIANS 10:3-5 (NET)

Scripture pulls the curtain back and shows us that there is a spiritual conflict in the universe. In this cosmic war, humans are often pawns. God's enemy, Satan, cannot hurt God. His unmatched power makes him unassailable.

What do you do when you can't hurt somebody? You hurt his children. Do you want to hurt me? Hurt my kids. Therefore, Satan tries to hurt you in his quest to hurt God. In fact, Satan wants to destroy you. He wants to destroy your relationships. He wants to destroy your finances. He wants to destroy your confidence in God's power. He wants to destroy your mental health. He wants to destroy your life.

That is the bad news. You were born into a battle. However, you happen to be on the winning side. John the Apostle says, "Greater is he who is in you than he who is in the world" (1 John 4:4). Satan is not afraid of you. He is afraid of who is in you. Therefore, if you have the Spirit of God, you don't have to be afraid of Satan.

Where does this leave those who don't know Christ? The evil one holds them imprisoned with powerful accusations. The most compelling in his arsenal is that God wants to coerce us into following him. God's enemy whispers, "He claims to be good and says he wants to give us good things; what he really wants to do is control us and put restrictions on everything we do."

God neutralized Satan's greatest accusation with the cross. Jesus' spectacular display of love not only paves a path toward reconciliation; it also prompts a free will response from us to draw near. The cross reveals that God is not an angry taskmaster who wants to control us. He's a God of love who wants to lavish us with good things.

The cross of Christ spelled Satan's downfall. At the final judgment, God will point to the cross as proof of the evil one's lies and evidence of his guilt. Satan's ultimate defeat has driven him to redouble his efforts. His blind rage has given him renewed motivation to prevent non-Christian people from ever hearing about Jesus or placing their faith in him. Satan knows his days are numbered, and he wants to see as many people as possible perish with him.

WHO IS OUR ENEMY?

Each day we see a news story that leaves us roiling or clenching our jaws. We say to ourselves, "I can't believe how insane and deluded our culture is becoming." As the world descends further into darkness and confusion, our outrage may mutate into contempt.

Those who parrot these false ideologies are not our enemies. The academics, politicians, celebrities and influencers who espouse these views aren't the minds behind these belief systems. They are the victims. The architect behind the values and ideas that deceive the world is Satan. He's our true enemy.

Jesus had the opposite reaction to the wickedness he witnessed. Matthew says that he saw the crowds and "had compassion on them" because they were "harassed and bewildered, like sheep without a shepherd" (Matthew 9:36). We must not view people in the world as enemies. We must view them as captives enslaved by God's enemy.

If you feel tempted to look down in disgust at the world around you, reflect on this. Where would you be without the illuminating presence of the Holy Spirit? Where would you be without the grace of God? What did God and his people do to rescue you out of the world?

Francis Schaeffer, one of the most prophetic voices in the 20th century, oozed compassion.

> Don't be proud. As you look out across the world of sinners, weep for them. Be glad indeed if you are redeemed, but never forget as you look at others that you have been one of them, and in a real sense we are still one with them, for we still sin. Christians are not a special group of people who can be proud; Christians are those who are redeemed — and that is all![51]

Becoming like Jesus means being a man or woman of sorrows and one who is well acquainted with grief over lost people. Our compassion for the fate of humanity apart from God should carry us forward to liberate those "who all their lives have been held in slavery to the fear of death" (Hebrews 2:15).

THE CHURCH AS AN ARMY

The New Testament uses a variety of metaphors such as a field, a radiant bride and a human body to describe the church. It also depicts the church as an army and believers as combatants in spiritual war (Ephesians 6:10-17; Matthew 16:18). We enlisted to serve as freedom fighters the moment we placed our faith in Jesus.

Churches that lose their sense of mission erect barricades of protection. They drift into seeing themselves as besieged on all sides by a degrading culture. That's why many churches try to shield their members from the world by calling them to embrace an alternative Christian subculture.

When the church sees its strategy as self-preservation, it departs from the vision God gives in the New Testament. Churches on the defensive are not only incapable of rescuing those under Satan's captivity; they also develop spiritual illnesses. Insular churches take up a self-righteous posture toward outsiders. In other cases, conflict devours these ingrown churches because they lack purpose.

THE WEAPONS OF OUR WARFARE

Unlike in human warfare, we don't engage our enemy with rifles. We wage war in the realm of ideas. Scripture teaches that we are tearing down the bulwark of beliefs that blocks people from knowing God. We accomplish this by countering each of Satan's lies and accusations with truth, or by bringing God's power to bear through prayer. These bring freedom to those whom Satan has entrapped with falsehoods and lies.

Yet, we can't tear down the evil one's strongholds with only intellectual arguments and persuasive speech. The weapons we use are not of this world. It's the power of God's word and prayer that bring clarity to people's thinking, like a beam of light that pierces into darkness.

Scripture calls on us to demolish arguments and every arrogant obstacle raised up against the knowledge of God. The expression "raised up" belongs to the world of ancient warfare and often referred to a tower or rampart. Cities often had a curtain wall that surrounded it. Towers flanked these walls, making it more difficult to capture the city. During a siege, archers would station themselves in these towers and attack climbing enemy soldiers. Thus, invading armies attacked the towers first, making it easier to breach the wall.

Following Paul's metaphor, "arguments" and "obstacles" make up these strongholds. Satan owns them, and we must batter them down. Several types of thinking must be demolished with truth and refutation.

Worldviews

Arguments raised up against the knowledge of God may take the form of religious views such as Buddhism, Hinduism and Animism. They can also take the form of philosophical worldviews: atheism, universalism and agnosticism. They may be an ideology that springs from one of these views. For example, materialism and hedonism flow from atheism. All of these -isms represent mental strongholds that contradict core truths of biblical faith.

Personal Attitudes

Distressing emotions may turn into mental strongholds. Worry can be one. So can fear. These negative emotions often prevent us from trusting God or experiencing his grace. They draw our eyes inward, highlighting our inadequacies, while diverting our attention from God. If these negative emotions persist, they turn into obstacles raised up against the knowledge of God.

Unique Struggles

Many in our culture feel as if the system is rigged against them because of their skin color, social class or sexual orientation. Historically, minority groups have faced more challenges than those of majority culture.

Many people wrestle with mental health issues and past abuse. These present unique challenges to spiritual growth. How do you help believers grow with God when they are extremely depressed? How do you come alongside individuals grappling with sexual abuse while directing them toward the truth in Scripture? There are no easy answers. We need to show sensitivity and patience toward those who face these struggles while calling on them to agree with God's word and take responsibility in areas they can control.

My Perception Is My Reality

This statement captures how many in our culture determine what's true. It's the lens through which people see their gender or sexuality. It's the lens through which people view disagreement or conflict. It's the lens through which people judge how others have treated them.

Social psychologist Jonathan Haidt and journalist Greg Lukianoff term this pattern of thinking the "Untruth of Emotional Reasoning." They state:

> Feelings are always compelling, but not always reliable. Often they distort reality, deprive us of insight, and needlessly damage our relationships… The feelings themselves are real, and sometimes they alert us to truths that our conscious mind has not noticed, but sometimes they lead us astray.[52]

"Don't believe everything you think," warns Christian author and speaker Rick Warren. He continues, "We naturally feel that if we think something, it must be true because it comes from within us. But just because you think something does not make it true."[53] Intrusive thoughts infiltrate our minds each day. Our culture bombards our minds with false ideas everywhere we turn. Why should we assume that if we think something, it must be true?

We also need to identify strongholds in other people's thinking. This starts with examining our own pattern of thinking. What ways have we have fallen for arguments and arrogant obstacles erected by Satan? It is impossible to see his strongholds if they are areas where we have a blind spot.

AN OPENING OF THE EYES

The most dangerous place to find yourself is on a battlefield with no idea of what's happening. Some of you lack awareness of the spiritual conflict taking place right here on earth. Simply learning about God's enemy and his tactics isn't enough. You need a spiritual opening of the eyes.

In the Old Testament, the King of Aram was searching for the prophet Elisha to kill him and surrounded the city where he was staying. When Elisha's servant woke up the next morning and found the city surrounded, he cried out to Elisha in fear.

> "Don't be afraid!" Elisha told him. "For there are more on our side than on theirs!"
>
> Then Elisha prayed, "O LORD, open his eyes and let him see!"
>
> The LORD opened the young man's eyes, and when he looked up, he saw that the hillside around Elisha was filled with horses and chariots of fire. (2 Kings 6:16-17)

Like Elisha's servant, we need an opening of the eyes to see that we are at the center of a spiritual conflict. Turn to God and ask him to reveal the battle raging all around you.

Sovereign Lord, open my eyes to see the spiritual battle in which we are engaged. Help me to see Satan's strongholds in my thinking and discern them in others. I pray that your compassion for those who are lost and imprisoned to the enemy's lies would move me to action. I pray that it would motivate me to devote myself to the church's mission in the world. Amen.

TWENTY-SEVEN
Combatant: The Battle of the Mind

> We demolish arguments and every pretension that sets itself
> up against the knowledge of God and we take captive every
> thought to make it obedient to Christ.
> **2 CORINTHIANS 10:5**

> Finally, brothers and sisters, whatever is true, whatever
> is noble, whatever is right, whatever is pure, whatever is
> lovely, whatever is admirable — if anything is excellent or
> praiseworthy — think about such things.
> **PHILIPPIANS 4:8**

> Therefore put on the full armor of God, so that when the day of
> evil comes, you may be able to stand your ground, and after
> you have done everything, to stand.
> **EPHESIANS 6:13**

Warfare doesn't just involve offensive maneuvers; it also requires an understanding of defensive tactics. Likewise, Satan will launch counter-offensives against God's people as they take critical ground for his kingdom.

God's enemy will attempt to neutralize the threat of believers freeing his captives. He does this through a variety of methods such as distraction, temptation, accusation and deception. The common element in each of his tactics is that they target our minds. God's enemy sees our weakness and exploits it. He knows that the Fall warped our minds and that we are not always in control of what thoughts enter them.

I've noticed that my mind doesn't always cooperate. It often disobeys me. It wants to go in a different direction. As I sit down to reflect, I notice my house is in a state of neglect. If I attempt to pray, my mind goes astray. This is why Paul urges believers to take every thought captive to the obedience of Christ (2 Corinthians 10:5).

Some thoughts and attitudes will overrun your mind if you don't take them captive. If you do not confront them, they can fester and infect your spiritual life. If left untreated, they will sideline us from the mission. Let's look at three steps you can take to win the battle.

COUNTER ACCUSATION WITH TRUTH

God's enemy follows three predictable lines of attack. He lobs charges at God, at us and at others. Each time a thought climbs into our heads that does not come from God, we must counter it with truth.

First, God's enemy accuses us to ourselves. In boxing, you use your jab to compromise your opponent's guard to set up a power punch. God's enemy will often tempt us into sin so that he can pummel us with accusation. The guilt we experience after sin causes us to feel shame, which seems like a wall between God and us. It creates alienation and blocks us from experiencing intimacy with him. It's vitally important, therefore, that we claim the truth of our new identity after a moral failure.

Paul tells us that God reconciled us through Jesus, so that he could present us perfect in his sight and free from accusation (Colossians 1:22). We can boldly declare, "Who will bring any charge against those whom God has chosen? It is God who justifies. Who then is the one who condemns?

No one. Christ Jesus who died — more than that, who was raised to life — is at the right hand of God and is also interceding for us" (Romans 8:33-34).

Second, Satan casts aspersions on other members in the body of Christ. He will exploit someone's anger to sow discord within the church. He knows he can weaken the church by dividing it. A group in crisis will devour itself, neutralizing its effectiveness for God. That's why God warns, "Do not let the sun go down while you are still angry, and do not give the devil a foothold" (Ephesians 4:26-27). Unresolved anger makes us vulnerable. Satan will cultivate seeds of anger so that bitterness will germinate in our hearts. When bitterness takes root, shoots of accusation blossom in our minds. We assign sinister motives to the words and actions of others, which further infuriates us.

Third, the evil one will accuse God to us. He will question God's goodness. Trial, hardship and suffering are breeding grounds for doubt and accusation. Thoughts such as *God has abandoned me* or, *He's not going to provide a spouse*, climb into your mind during times of emotional distress. Paul responds to these accusations, "What, then, shall we say in response to these things? If God is for us, who can be against us? He who did not spare his own Son, but gave him up for us all — how will he not also, along with him, graciously give us all things?" (Romans 8:31-32).

It's important to reiterate that we cannot outwit or outmatch God's enemy. We must rely on the power of God's word to protect us. In the book of Ephesians, the Apostle Paul urges us to be ready to defend ourselves:

> Therefore put on the full armor of God, so that when the day of evil comes, you may be able to stand your ground…Stand firm then, with the belt of truth buckled around your waist, with the breastplate of righteousness in place, and with your feet fitted with the readiness that comes from the gospel of peace. In addition to all this, take up the shield of faith, with which you can extinguish all the flaming arrows of the evil one. (Ephesians 6:13-16)

We cannot extinguish the evil one's flaming arrows if we are not equipped. Notice how each piece of armor relates to the truth found in God's word and our new identity in Jesus. This means we need to put in the hard work of learning God's word and memorizing Scripture related to our standing in Christ.

PREVENT INGRATITUDE FROM SPOILING YOUR JOY

Some of us are facing trials and hardships. Others of us are working a job we don't like. Still others are struggling as new parents. It's easy to fall into a mindset where we feel as if we deserve better because we've devoted our lives to serving the Lord.

Ingratitude and grumbling rob us of the joy in the Christian life — replacing it with soul-grinding obligation. Pastor Tim Keller in his book, *Prayer*, argues that the essence of sin is neither glorifying God nor giving thanks. External forces often drive us to prayer. When we fall into sin, we repent to God and ask for restoration. When a family member gets a shocking diagnosis, we plead with God for healing. What happens when life is going well? You would expect that this would provoke thanksgiving and praise in the same way bad things move us to petition and intercession. Yet it often doesn't.

Romans 1:21 describes the heart of human sin: "For although they knew God, they neither glorified him as God nor gave thanks to him." Failing to glorify God and give him thanks? That's the essence of sin? Yes, it is. To illustrate this point, Keller uses the analogy of plagiarism:

> Why is plagiarism taken so seriously? It is claiming that you came up with an idea yourself when you did not. It is not acknowledging dependence, that you got the idea from someone else. Plagiarism is a refusal to give thanks and give credit and is, therefore, a form of theft. It not only wrongs the author of the idea — it also puts you in a vulnerable position, because you are not capable of producing such ideas yourself in the future.[54]

Likewise, failing to give thanks to God amounts to taking credit for the good things he has given us. It's robbing God of his glory. Ingratitude is also the delusion of self-sufficiency. Keller comments on this:

> It is taking credit for something that was a gift. It is the belief that you know best how to live, that you have the power and ability to keep your life on the right path and protect yourself from danger. That is a delusion, and a dangerous one…We are never as thankful as we should be. When good things come to us, we do everything possible to tell ourselves we accomplished that or at least deserve it. We take the credit. And when our lives simply are going along pretty smoothly, without a lot of difficulties, we don't live in quiet, amazed, thankful consciousness of it.[55]

No wonder Paul tells us to make a habit of reflecting on God's goodness and generosity: "Whatever is true, whatever is noble, whatever is right, whatever is pure, whatever is lovely, whatever is admirable — if anything is excellent or praiseworthy — think about such things" (Philippians 4:8). Taking an inventory of good things God has given us and expressing gratitude for them are acts of humility. They give God the credit and acknowledge our dependence on him.

BE CAREFUL WHAT FILLS YOUR MIND

Dieticians will tell you that there are three broad types of food. Healthy foods that are nutrient-rich and high in protein. Foods that offer empty calories and contain little nutritional value. And foods that are bad for you that are high in saturated fat and sugar.

Your genetics may put you at risk for high blood pressure or high cholesterol. You can't control that. But you can control what you put in your body. It's the same with your mind. You can't always control what comes into your mind, but you can control what you put into it. Proverbs 15:14 says, "A wise person is hungry for knowledge, while the fool feeds on trash."

We can fill our minds with good things that advance or challenge our thinking, such as God's word or great works of literature. We can fill our minds with things that aren't bad, but perhaps not necessary, such as trivia or useless information. And then you have things that are not good for you, such as pornography or racist propaganda.

There are things that you should only consume in moderation. To use our food analogy again, there's nothing wrong with eating cheeseburgers and fried chicken from time to time. But you should not eat this stuff for lunch and dinner most days. The same goes for things like social media or news consumption. Some of us can't help scrolling through articles, looking for hourly updates about what's happening in our world. It's almost compulsive.

In 1978, famous Soviet dissident Aleksandr Solzhenitsyn delivered the Harvard University commencement address. In it, he critiqued American culture:

> "Everyone is entitled to know everything." (But this is a false slogan of a false era. Far greater in value is the forfeited right of people not to know, not to have their divine souls stuffed with gossip, nonsense, vain talk. A person who works and leads a meaningful life has no need for this excessive and burdening flow of information.)
>
> Hastiness and superficiality — these are the psychic diseases of the twentieth century...[56]

Solzhenitsyn's words have never been more true than they are today. The "forfeited right not to know" represents our culture's obsession to know everything in real time. It isn't a desire to remain informed — it's the "psychic disease of the twentieth century." The glut of news and information agitates our anxiety and fuels our anger.

Kelly McGonigal, a professor of psychology at Stanford University, points out, "In one major U.S. survey, exposure to the news was one of the most common sources of daily stress. Of people who reported high levels of stress, 40 percent mentioned watching, reading or listening to the news as a major contributor to the stress in their lives."[57] In one shocking study, researchers found: "People who watched six or more hours of news about the 2013 Boston Marathon bombing were more likely to develop post-traumatic stress symptoms than people who were at the bombing."[58]

Some of us consume news throughout the day — all in the name of staying informed. The thought is that if I know the latest news about what's happening in the world, then I'll be in a better position to protect myself and my family. This seems rational. But most people read the news well past the point of gathering useful information. These sessions often begin by scanning articles but end up with us scrolling through the comments section where people hurl insults at each other and say hateful things for shock value. We often catch ourselves and wonder, *Why am I reading this?* Rather than feeling calm and more prepared, we end these sessions feeling more anxious and inflamed with anger about something new.

PROTECTING OUR MINDS

As with anything in the spiritual life, we don't see permanent change by gritting our teeth and resisting our impulses. We must replace bad patterns with something positive. God exhorts believers to "flee the evil desires of youth and pursue righteousness, faith, love and peace" (2 Timothy 2:22). In other words, we must resist sinful desires and replace them with godly character and action.

Don't just restrict what fills your mind. Feed it with content that will challenge your thinking. Scripture does not merely affirm what you already think or believe — it stretches and corrects it. It's the only reliable external standard by which you can judge your thoughts and ideas.

Push yourself to read more. Set a yearly goal for how many books you plan to finish. Don't just read for entertainment. Read challenging content that requires sustained concentration.

Create mental space for reflection and critical thinking. These are perishable skills. If you don't take a disciplined approach to limiting your input and allowing your mind to process information, then you will suffer.

These practical suggestions will help you furnish your interior life with depth and insight. If you neglect them, self-examination will become scary. You will grow uncomfortable with quiet moments. Socrates, the famous ancient philosopher, once said, "The unexamined life is not worth living."[59]

Time accelerates as you get older because each year is a smaller fraction of your life. It's important, therefore, to stop and reflect on what God is teaching you. Otherwise, life will speed past, and you will have no clue what happened.

Lord, I find it difficult to take hold of thoughts. My commitment to serve you often feels at odds with my thoughts and my desires. Please, transform my mind and my affections so that they will not hinder my effectiveness for you. Teach me how to grow in my mental discipline and help me identify thoughts and attitudes that I must confront with your word. I pray these things in your son's name. Amen.

TWENTY-EIGHT
Conformed to the Image of Christ

I want to know Christ — yes, to know the power of his resurrection and participation in his sufferings, becoming like him in his death.
PHILIPPIANS 3:10

For those God foreknew he also predestined to be conformed to the image of his Son, that he might be the firstborn among many brothers and sisters.
ROMANS 8:29

We've come to our last day and the end of this book. This topic is a fitting end, since God's goal in spiritual growth is to transform us into the image of his son. He starts this restoration process the moment we place our faith in Jesus. The Spirit indwells us and changes us from the inside out. Over time, we take on characteristics that Jesus displayed.

Jesus lived a perfect life. He fulfilled the Law without faltering at even one point. He modeled dependence — relying on God the Father every moment of each day during his entire time on earth. His life was not just an exception to our broken human existence; Jesus embodied the life God intended us to live prior to the Fall.

It would be impossible to give a brief description of Jesus' qualities that would do them justice. The final line of John's gospel admits that his best attempt was far from complete: "There are many other things that Jesus did. If every one of them were written down, I suppose the whole world would not have room for the books that would be written" (John 21:25). We will spend the rest of eternity covering our mouths in astonishment of Jesus' radiant glory. We will plumb the depths of God's love for us as we look at what Jesus did for us on the cross. So we will not attempt to sketch a picture of Jesus' character in just a few pages.

Instead, we will look at the fruit God's Spirit produces in us that Jesus exemplified during his earthly ministry. Paul gives this list in Galatians 5:22-23: "The fruit of the Spirit is love, joy, peace, patience, kindness, goodness, faithfulness, gentleness and self-control." These qualities serve as a measure of maturity.

LOVE

Love distinguishes the Christian worldview from all others. Other religions regard love as a virtue. It stands on the periphery compared to ritual observances or religious discipline. Jesus pointed to the centrality of love when an expert of the Law asked him to identify the greatest commandment.

> "'Love the Lord your God with all your heart and with all your soul and with all your mind.' This is the first and greatest commandment. And the second is like it: 'Love your neighbor as yourself.' All the Law and the Prophets hang on these two commandments." (Matthew 22:37-40)

Love is such a pronounced feature of God's character that the Apostle John was able to say, "God is love" (1 John 4:8). It was out of love for us that God sent Jesus. Thus, we become more loving as we become more like Jesus. God delivers us from lives of selfishness and turns us into servants.

Love is the true measure of spirituality. The best way to gauge your progress is to examine the way you treat others. Serving others in love is the ultimate expression of Christ-likeness.

JOY

"Joy isn't a feeling — it's a choice." This odd sentiment captures a long tradition of Christian teaching. For example, one writer states, "We don't get joy by seeking a better emotional life, because joy is not an emotion. It is a settled certainty that God is in control."[60] Another claims, "Joy is distinctly a Christian word and a Christian thing. It is the reverse of happiness."[61] Does this fit with what Scripture says?

Randy Alcorn's book, *Happiness*, topples this long-standing view. Alcorn supplies a mountain of evidence arguing that the Greek word often translated "joy" should, in most cases, be translated "happy."[62]

You might ask, "Why does this matter?" Let me give you three reasons.

First, the human heart strives for happiness. L. K. Washburn once said, "Everybody wants to be happy, and thinks, strives, wishes, and lives to that end."[63] That's often why people come to Christ. They're unhappy with their lives. Second, no one would become a Christian if following God didn't make people happy. Imagine someone came up to you and said, "Hey, I have a suggestion: You should put your faith in something that is going to make you more depressed, anxious and miserable." What kind of offer is that? Finally, dour, mopey Christians leave people with the wrong impression about God. Many non-Christian people use words such as "judgmental" and "hateful" to describe Jesus' followers. These words describe unhappy people.

God wants us to serve with joy. He does not want us to give the impression that following him is about tight-jawed self-sacrifice. Mature believers exude gratitude to God for all he has given. They seem content and happy with their lives. Even trials and hardships do not extinguish their hope. They mirror Jesus, who "for the joy set before him he endured the cross, scorning its shame, and sat down at the right hand of the throne of God" (Hebrews 12:2).

PEACE

The Fall put us at odds with ourselves. Worry and anxiety consume our minds. But Jesus promises to give his followers peace. Not the kind the world offers, but peace with God that permeates every dimension of life. God's active presence enables us to experience a type of inner peace that transcends understanding.

It mends rifts that divide people, too. It's the basis for racial unity, closeness within the church and reconciliation in our relationships. As mentioned earlier, our mystical union with Christ gives us a basis for peace in our relationships. We should also be agents of peace, brokering it between God and men and among God's people (Matthew 5:9).

PATIENCE

God endures our rebellion and sinfulness. He shows great patience with us, even though we deserve judgment. The Apostle Peter explains that the reason the Lord has not returned and restored justice is because "he is patient with you, not wanting anyone to perish, but everyone to come to repentance" (2 Peter 3:9). The Greek word Peter uses is a compound term meaning "long-anger." God is just, but he has a long fuse. He is slow to judge.

The Apostle Paul presents his life as proof of God's patience. This becomes clear as you track the comments he makes about himself in the New Testament. In his first admission, he insists, "I am the least of all the apostles" (1 Corinthians 15:9). Five years later, he goes even further: "I am less than the least of all the Lord's people" (Ephesians 3:8). A couple of years before his death, he declares, "I am the worst of all sinners"

(1 Timothy 1:15). As you mature in Christ, there's a growing sense of unworthiness and a growing sense of confidence in God's love.

That's why Paul asserts: "God had mercy on me so that Christ Jesus could use me as a prime example of his great patience with even the worst sinners" (1 Timothy 1:16).

Paul acted in ignorance, persecuting and even killing Christians. He convinced himself he was doing God's will. To his shock, he encountered the risen Jesus and discovered he was opposing God and his purposes.

Modern people interpret Paul calling himself "the worst sinner" as a form of self-hatred. This is one of the reasons why they balk at the Christian worldview. They see Paul branding himself a sinner as evidence that Christianity encourages people to feel shame.

Scripture teaches the opposite. Admitting your fault will not lead to shame. It brings freedom and an opportunity to experience God's love in a new way. His mercy frees us from our true moral guilt, which takes away the object of our shame. This gives you a deeper appreciation for God's grace. As you grow in awareness of God's loving endurance toward you, you will show more of it toward others.

KINDNESS AND GOODNESS

Kindness denotes a friendly disposition, and goodness speaks to one's virtue. The Greek words behind these terms, however, suggest more. They describe the positive moral quality of generosity and a strong interest in the welfare of others. As God transforms you into the image of Christ, you become less self-absorbed and more sacrificial. He rewires your mind so that your default mode isn't to "merely look out for your own personal interests," and you start to consider "the interests of others" (Philippians 2:4). Jesus possessed this outlook. He did not come to earth for people to serve him; rather, he came to give his life for others.

FAITHFULNESS

This quality describes someone you would regard as reliable and trustworthy. It's the same word Jesus uses to describe a faithful servant (Luke 16:9). It's someone who shows consistency in the area of serving.

It also refers to someone who perseveres. Life contains many trials that will test your faith. These hardships may push you to the brink of quitting. Those conformed to the image of Jesus persevere through suffering with joy. They recognize that following Jesus is not a sprint; it's a marathon. It's a test of endurance.

GENTLENESS

Jesus describes himself as "gentle and humble of heart" (Matthew 11:29). And Paul attributes the same character qualities to Jesus when he appeals to the Corinthians with "the humility and gentleness of Christ" (2 Corinthians 10:1).

This seems to contradict other pictures of Jesus in the New Testament. For example, Jesus cleared the Temple courts of predatory money lenders and vendors selling marked up sacrificial animals (John 2). He drove animals from their stalls with a whip fashioned from cords. He flipped over money tables and flung the coins to the floor. In the book of Revelation, the Apostle John describes Jesus as a king who releases the fury of God. Thus, you cannot equate Jesus' gentleness and humility with weakness.

We need to see both sides. He's not just our friend; he's also a king. We should never mistake God's kindness with weakness or his patience with permissiveness.

Ancient authors sometimes used the Greek word for gentle to describe the taming of a wild animal.[64] This may give us insight into what Jesus meant when he described himself as gentle. Horses are powerful beasts. A wild horse cannot distinguish a human from a predator and will buck a person off its back or kick them in confined spaces. This could result in serious injuries, even death. By contrast, a tamed horse may appear gentle and domesticated; yet, it still has the strength of a mustang. In the same way, Jesus accepted the limitations of human flesh even though he possessed God's infinite power. He set aside the use of his divine might during his earthly ministry.

Gentleness is power under restraint. You may have a strong will, which expresses itself in either defiance or obstinance. God will not strip you of it and turn you into a servile person as he conforms you to the image of Christ. He can repurpose a strong will. He directs it from always trying to get your way and toward serving others or advocating for the needs of the poor. He teaches you how to defer to others, not out of fear of conflict, but out of humility and mutual submission. In time, family and close friends will notice how you showed unusual restraint in situations where they expected you to react with a show of force.

SELF-CONTROL

Jesus restricted his divinity by putting on humanity. That means he possessed the same drives and desires we feel. He was "tempted in every way, just as we are — yet he did not sin" (Hebrews 4:15). Jesus was able to control his impulses and appetites.

You might say, "Well, Jesus did not have a sin nature." That's not an explanation for succumbing to sin, however. The first humans did not have a sin nature.

Scripture tells us we are no longer slaves to sin. Prior to knowing Christ, we did not have the willpower to resist sinful desires. Now that we have the Spirit of God, we have a force that counteracts our sinful nature. That's why we feel an internal struggle between the Spirit and our sinful nature (Galatians 5:17). The more we walk in step with the Holy Spirit's leading, over time we will find ourselves giving into our sinful tendencies less.

GOD'S PART AND OUR PART

Spiritual transformation is not a passive process. God's power is the driving force behind your growth, but you play an important role. The Lord calls on you to work out your spiritual growth while he is "working in you, giving you the desire and the power to do what pleases him" (Philippians 2:12-13, NLT). God will transform your mind and values if you develop the habit of regular prayer and Scripture study. He will expose relational tendencies and character flaws as you spend quality time with other believers and try to serve. And he will deepen your faith as you learn to trust him through suffering. Our progress toward Christlike character is a joint venture: We put in the effort, God supplies the power.

Heavenly Father, you are faithful even when we are faithless. You are committed to our spiritual growth, even when we resist change or fail to take our part in it seriously. Thank you for the ways you have changed our lives. We know that we will be like Christ the moment we see him. In the meantime, I pray that you would continue your work of conforming us to the image of your son, Jesus. We pray that the difference people see in us would bring glory to your name. Amen.

ENDNOTES

A Simple Solution to a Complex Problem

1. Sara Solnick and David Hemenway, "Is More Always Better?: A Survey on Positional Concerns," *Journal of Economic Behavior and Organization* 37, no. 3 (Nov 1998): 373-383. These figures have been adjusted for 2022 inflation.

2. Timothy Keller, *Counterfeit Gods: The Empty Promises of Money, Sex, Power, and the Only Hope That Matters* (London: Penguin Publishing Group, 2011), 5.

Seeing Yourself Through God's Eyes

3. Albrecht Oepke, "Βάπτω," in *Theological Dictionary of the New Testament*, ed. Gerhard Kittel, Geoffrey W. Bromiley, and Gerhard Friedrich (Grand Rapids, MI: Eerdmans, 1964), 1:542.

4. Dennis McCallum, *Walking in Victory: Why God's Love Can Change Your Life Like Legalism Never Could* (Columbus, Ohio: New Paradigm Publishing, 2012), 16.

Free from the Law

5. Cornelius Plantinga, Jr., *Not the Way It's Supposed to Be* (Grand Rapids, MI: Eerdmans Publishing, 1995), 171.

6. For a great treatment on this subject, see Tim Keller's book *Prodigal God*.

7. Richard Lovelace, *Dynamics of Spiritual Life* (Downers Grove, IL: Inter-Varsity Press, 1979), 212.

8. McCallum, *Walking in Victory*, 56.

No Longer Slaves to Sin

9. Timothy Keller, *Making Sense of God: Finding God in the Modern World* (New York: Penguin Publishing Group, 2018), 99-100.

10. Ibid.

11. See the origins of the Juneteenth celebration where Maj. Gen. Gordon Granger announced the emancipation of slaves in Galveston, Texas, two and a half years after Lincoln signed the Emancipation Proclamation.

12. Neil T. Anderson, *Victory Over the Darkness: 10th Anniversary Edition* (Ventura, California: Gospel Light, 2000), Location 1505, Kindle.

13. David M. Oshinsky, *Worse than Slavery: Parchman Farm and the Ordeal of Jim Crow Justice* (New York: Free Press, 1997), 17.

Forgiven

14. This insight comes from Tim Keller's 2008 sermon on Matthew 18 entitled, "Forgiveness and Reconciliation."

15. Miroslav Volf, *Exclusion and Embrace: Revised and Updated* (Nashville, TN: Abingdon Press, 2019), 124, Kindle.

16. Frederick Buechner, *Wishful Thinking: A Theological ABC* (New York: Harper & Row, 1973), 2.

17. Dan Hamilton, *Forgiveness* (Westmont, IL: IVP, 1980), 10.

Adopted Son or Daughter

18. According to Francis Lyall, this concept wasn't wholly unknown in Jewish practice. He cites the parable of the Prodigal Son as an example. However, he notes particular differences. The father gives the Prodigal Son his share of the inheritance and the son leaves without any change in his legal status as heir. This would not have been possible under Roman law. An heir would have to gain emancipation from the head of the family to receive a share of the property. By doing so, the son would forfeit his status as an heir. For a more in-depth treatment of this topic, see Francis Lyall's *Slaves, Citizens, Sons: Legal Metaphors in the Epistles* chapter on adoption.

19. Justinian's *Digest of Roman Law* states, "On the death of the father the heirs are not seen to inherit the property as rather to acquire the free control of their own property" (D. 28.2.11).

20. Modern Greek speakers use this word refer to an engagement ring.

21. F. F. Bruce reminds us that we must interpret the implications of our adoption in terms of the Greco-Roman culture of Paul's day. He writes, "The term 'adoption' may have a somewhat artificial sound in our ears; but in the Roman world of the first century A.D. an adopted son was a son deliberately chosen by his adoptive father to perpetuate his name and inherit his estate." *Romans,* Tyndale New Testament Commentary (Westmont, IL: InterVarsity Press, 2008), 36.

Child of God: Our Heavenly Father

22. Keller, *Making Sense of God,* 129.

Child of God: Receiving Loving Discipline

23. Randy Alcorn, *Happiness* (Carol Stream, IL: Tyndale House Publishers, 2015), 202, Kindle.

God's Friend

24. Lydia Saad and Zach Hrynowski, "How Many Americans Believe in God," *Gallup,* June 24, 2022, https://news.gallup.com/poll/268205/americans-believe-god.aspx.

God's Friend: Being a Good Friend

25. Aristotle, *Nicomachean Ethics,* trans. W.D. Ross, The Internet Classics Archive, Book VIII.7, http://classics.mit.edu/Aristotle/nicomachaen.8.viii.html.

26. John White, *Excellence in Leadership* (Downers Grove, IL: InterVarsity Press, 1986), 24, Kindle.

27. Timothy Keller, *Prayer* (New York: Penguin Publishing Group, 2014), 53.

28. Timothy Ward, *Words of Life: Scripture as the Living and Active Word of God* (Downers Grove, IL: InterVarsity Press, 2009), 31.

29. Gallup Organization, Gallup News Service Poll: January 1990, Wave 2, Gallup Organization, (Cornell University, Ithaca, NY: Roper Center for Public Opinion Research, 1990), Dataset, DOI: 10.25940/ROPER-31088676.

30. Daniel A. Cox, "The State of American Friendship: Change, Challenges, and Loss," *Survey Center on American Life*, June 8, 2021, https://www.americansurveycenter. org/research/the-state-of-american-friendship-change-challenges-and-loss/.

31. Keller, *Prayer*, 46.

32. Rick Warren, *The Purpose Driven Life: What On Earth Am I Here For?* (Grand Rapids, MI: Zondervan, 2012), 96.

Bearer of God's Family Name

33. Robert Bellah et al., *Habits of the Heart* (Los Angeles, CA: University of California Press, 1985), 334–35.

34. Keller, *Making Sense of God*, 127.

35. Ibid., 102.

One in Christ

36. Brad Christerson, Korie L. Edwards, and Michael O. Emerson, *Against All Odds: The Struggle for Racial Integration in Religious Organizations* (New York: NYU Press, 2005), 151-52.

Bride of Christ

37. John R. W. Stott, *God's New Society: The Message of Ephesians.* The Bible Speaks Today. (Downers Grove, IL: InterVarsity Press, 1979), 228.

Royal Priesthood

38. Francis Schaeffer, *The Complete Works of Francis A. Schaeffer: A Christian Worldview* (Wheaton, IL: Crossway Books, 1982), 1:112.

39. David G. Peterson, *Engaging with God: A Biblical Theology of Worship* (Downers Grove, IL: Intervarsity Press, 1992), 18.

Salt + Light

40. D. A. Carson, "Matthew," in *The Expositor's Bible Commentary*, ed. Frank E. Gaebelein (Grand Rapids, MI: Zondervan Publishing House, 1984), 8: 138.

Citizen of Heaven

41. Alan F. Johnson, "Revelation," in *The Expositor's Bible Commentary*, ed. Frank E.

Gaebelein (Grand Rapids, MI: Zondervan Publishing House, 1981), 12: 449.

42. C.S. Lewis, *The Problem of Pain* (New York: Harper Collins, 2009), 145-150.

Temporary Resident

43. Minucius Felix, "Octavius," *The Ante-Nicene Fathers*, trans. R. E. Wallis (Buffalo, NY: The Christian Literature Publishing Co., 1887), 4: 177-178.

44. Karen H. Jobes, *1 Peter,* Baker Exegetical Commentary on the New Testament (Grand Rapids, MI: Baker Academic, 2022), 170.

45. Julian, "Letter to Arsacius," in *Julian: Letters, Epigrams, Against the Galilaeans, Fragments,* trans. Wilmer C. Wright. (Cambridge, MA: Harvard University Press, 1923), III: 429C.

Ambassador

46. This illustration about Ugly Americans comes from Gary Delashmutt's teaching on 2 Corinthians 6:1-11. https://teachings.dwellcc.org/teaching/705

47. Watchman Nee, *The Normal Christian Worker* (Hong Kong: Hong Kong Church Book Room Ltd., 1971), 18.

Not of This World

48. Michael Luo, "American Christianity's White-Supremacy Problem," *New Yorker,* September 2, 2020, https://www.newyorker.com/books/under-review/american-christianitys-white-supremacy-problem.

Servant of Christ

49. Rich Warren, "Focus on Living for an Audience of One," *Daily Hope Devotional,* October 19, 2020, https://pastorrick.com/focus-on-living-for-an-audience-of-one.

50. Robert Coleman, *The Master Plan of Evangelism* (Grand Rapids, MI: Revell Publishing, 1963), 37.

Combatant: Freedom Fighter

51. Francis Schaeffer, *Genesis in Space and Time* (Westmost, IL: InterVarsity Press, 2009), 90.

52. Greg Lukianoff and Jonathan Haidt, *Coddling of the American Mind: How Good Intentions and Bad Ideas Are Setting Up a Generation for Failure* (New York: Penguin Books, 2018), 34-35.

53. Rick Warren, "The Battle for Your Mind," *Desiring God,* October 1, 2010, https://www.desiringgod.org/messages/the-battle-for-your-mind.

Combatant: The Battle of the Mind

54. Keller, *Prayer,* 196.

55. Ibid.

56. Aleksandr Solzhenitsyn, "A World Split Apart," *The Aleksandr Solzhenitsyn Center*, https://www.solzhenitsyncenter.org/a-world-split-apart.

57. Kelly McGonigal, *The Upside of Stress* (New York: Penguin Publishing, 2015), 133.

58. E. Alison Holman, Dana Rose Garfin, and Roxane Cohen Silver, "Media's Role In Broadcasting Acute Stress Following the Boston Marathon Bombings," *PNAS 111, no. 1* (Nov 2013), 93-98.

59. Plato, "The Apology," in *Plato*, trans. H.N. Fowler (New York: The Macmillan Co., 1913), 38a5-6.

Conformed to the Image of Christ

60. Greg Forster, *The Joy of Calvinism: Knowing God's Personal, Unconditional, Irresistible, Unbreakable Love* (Wheaton, IL: Crossway, 2012), 147–48.

61. S. D. Gordon, quoted in Billy Graham, *Peace with God: The Secret Happiness* (Nashville: Thomas Nelson, 2000), 202.

62. See Randy Alcorn, *Happiness* (Carol Stream, IL: Tyndale House Publishers, 2015), 176-256. The Greek word for "rejoice" (chara/chairō) could be translated "be happy" or "be glad." Look at an earlier example in Philippians 2:27-30. In the context, Paul is telling the Philippians that he is sending Epaphroditus, who nearly died of an illness. "I am all the more eager to send [Epaphroditus], so that when you see him again you may be [chairo] *glad* and I may have less anxiety. So then, welcome him in the Lord with [*chara*] *great joy*, and honor people like him, because he almost died for the work of Christ. Clearly, Paul was talking about an emotion here. He wasn't talking about a "settled certainty that God is in control." It's happiness that Epaphroditus didn't die.

63. L. K. Washburn, "Helps to Happiness," *Freethinker* 18, part 2, July 24, 1898, 474.

64. Xenophon, "Cyropaedia," in *Xenophon in Seven Volumes*, trans. Walter Miller (Cambridge, MA: Harvard University Press, 1914), 5: II,1,29.

SEARCHING
FOR WISDOM
FINDING THE FATHER IN PROVERBS
CONRAD HILARIO